THE GULAG TRAIL

FOOTPRINTS INTO EXILE

Copyright © 2014 Our Roots Trust

"Our Roots Trust" is a Charitable Trust registered with the
Charities Commission for England and Wales
No. 1140623

Published on "CreateSpace Independent Publishing Platform"

Editing by Pamela Brown MA
Cover design by Pamela Brown
All rights reserved

ISBN 13:978-1502851529

ISBN 10:1502851520

DEDICATION

In memory of my father and all those who left their footprints on the road into exile

A Note from the Author

 I was born in 1939 in what was then Poland, and is now Belarus. I grew up a happy boy in India oblivious of the carnage of WW2 and came to the UK in 1947 for the family to be reunited with my father serving in General Anders' Polish 2nd Corps.

Only very much later in my life I learned of the horrors of our family's deportation to Siberia in April 1940, the death of my little sister in Tehran on the way to our freedom, my father's years in Stalin's GULAG camps and our saviour, General Anders, who led so many Polish people out of Russia. I knew nothing in those early years of my father's participation in the battle for Monte Cassino, and the bitterness and grief of the Polish people at the loss of their Homeland to the Communist regime.

Poland, after WW2, for our family was closed; we could only expect prison for my father and persecution for the rest of us. So I grew up and grew old in the UK; I have lived and worked in the USA and in France for a number of years yet, each time, I returned to the UK – this was my homeland, the only home I knew.

In a much belated recognition of my parents' struggle and sacrifice I set out on a journey to feel the history of those years, and to pass it on to my children and grandchildren. Over the past ten years I have travelled with a backpack in Western Europe, Belarus, Ukraine, Uzbekistan and, in this book, searched for the footprints of the GULAG across Russia and Kazakhstan.

"The GULAG Trail" is the second of my stories on the theme "In the Footsteps of Our Fathers" to be published in support of the Charity, "Our Roots Trust" of which I am a founder member.

My sincere thanks to Ivan Vdovin for enabling me to visit GULAG-72km.; to Rafał Orłowski for his kind permission to quote extracts from his father's, Major Jan Orłowski, memoirs; to Alexander Kalmykov for showing me around Workuta; to Margarita Krotchik for the photographs from her personal album of work and life in GULAG Workuta; and to Victor for showing me around Abez and for the photographs of its history..

I would also like to express my thanks to Pamela Brown for the encouragement and support she gave me in the writing of my story, and my appreciation of her editorial comments and suggestions.

October 2014

Contents

Explanatory Notes	i
Preface	ii
Maps	iii
Illustrations on pages	27-29
Illustrations on pages	117-124
Illustrations on pages	180-184
1. Return of the "Prodigal Son"	5
2. Into Oblivion	15
3. Footprints in Russia	30
Workuta	38
Abez	48
Uhta - Yarega - Sangaradok	55
4. Footprints in Kazakhstan	68
Kingir Rudnik	70
Fedorovka-Karaganda	73
Spaask-Karaganda	76
5. *Tut Washa Moghila* – It's your grave	79
GULAG-72km.	82
Kirovsk	90
Revda	93
Valley of Death – Murmansk	96
The Ponoi *lagier*	102

6. *Szli do Armii* – to join the Army	125
Tockoye	138
Buzuluk	140
7. Deliverance or Death	145
8. Exit by the Cemetery	150
Aralsk	157
Krasnyy Most	159
Tashkent, YangiYul	165
Ghuzar	169
Epilogue	179
Sources & Works Cited	185
Bibliography	186

Explanatory Notes

arba – a wooden cart with flat bottom mounted on wooden wheels 6-8 feet in diameter.

chay - tea

NKVD – National Committee for Internal Affairs within the Soviet Union (the Soviet secret police from 1934-1946)

kipiatok – boiling water for making tea (chay)

kolkhoz (kolkhozes) – a co-operative farm in Soviet times where members are paid in kind, and not money, at the end of the year according to the number of days they had worked.

lagier (lagiers) - In everyday usage today, the word *lagier* means a camp. It could be a school camp, a holiday camp or any other camp, but in the context of the GULAG system, it means a concentration camp, a hard-labour camp.

nachalnik – the head of an organization, in this case the boss of the *lagier*.

posiolek – a village

refusnik – a person that refuses to comply with,

speclag – is a GULAG *lagier* with specially adverse and restrictive rules usually meant for prisoners sentenced to hard labour for political reasons.

Samovar – Russian traditional coal-fired kettle for boiling water to make tea.

Stolypin – Prime Minister in the last days of Imperial Russia whose name is associated with a particular type of wagons for prisoners

Volkesdeutsh – a person of German origin

GULAG – the main administrative body for the management of *lagiers* within the Soviet Union.

wyshka – a tower, here a guard tower in a *lagier*.

Preface

My father left home at the end of August 1939 to fight for Poland – I was six months old then. Eight years later, a man in "khaki and black beret" appeared in my life; my mother said he was my - daddy.

He was a military man and, in his eyes, I could neither stand up straight, nor squat or walk properly. We moved from one resettlement camp in the UK to another and lived our separate ways: he toiled on building sites to keep our family in daily bread, I "toiled" at my studies.

Sadly, my father died at the age of sixty-six, much too soon for me to put my arm around him and ask about the War. What could I know about war, about GULAG, about life in *lagiers* in Ponoi, or Workuta, Uhta or Abez? Or about the impact on man's mind of years of war and suffering?

But this ambiguous relationship between me and my father must have weighed on my mind for, many years later, I set out "In the Footsteps of Our Fathers" trailing the path fate had led him and so many other Polish fathers. I was looking for my missing "Daddy" and after ten years of searching for his footprints in Stalin's evil empire, I am beginning to "understand" and regret that it is now fifty years too late to ask him and listen to his story.

Maps

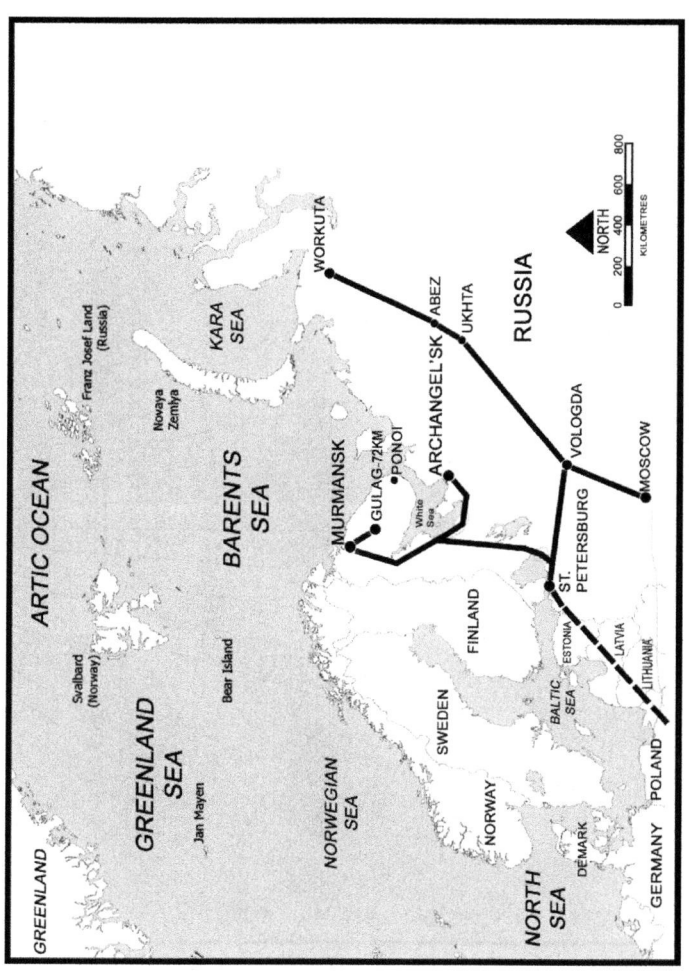

RUSSIA
Continuous lines show my GULAG Trail
Dashed line is the connecting flight from Warsaw.

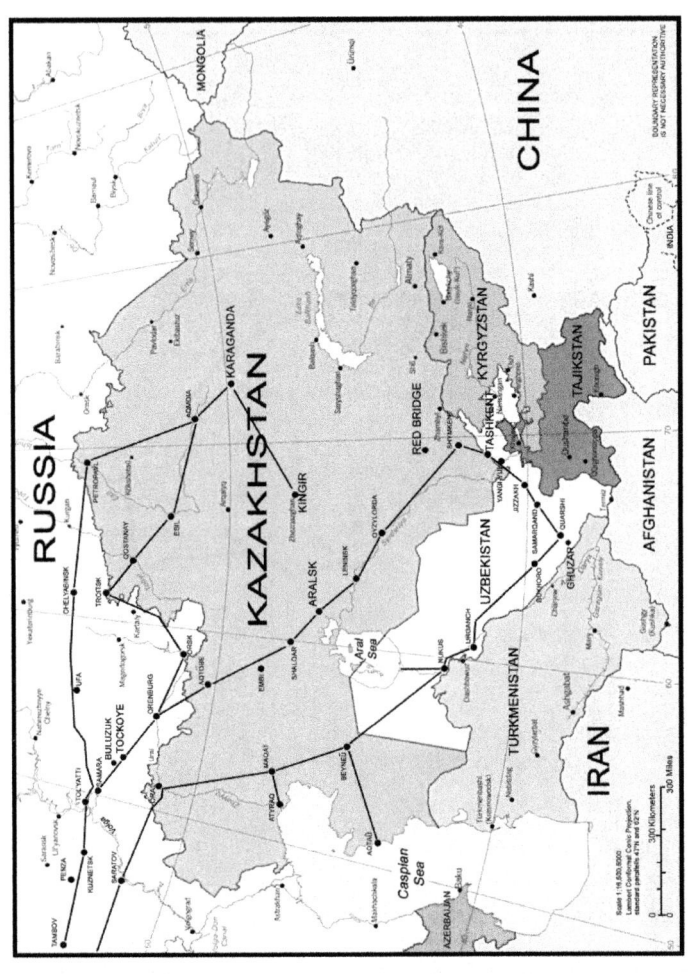

KAZAKHSTAN - UZBEKISTAN
Superimposed lines show my GULAG Trail

1

Return of the "Prodigal Son"

How can I explain it if I don't understand it myself?

The first time I visited Poland was in 1965 – for my wedding. Next - in 1973; I went there on business and continued going there a number of times a year. From 1993 onwards, I was spending as much as two weeks per month in Poland, and I cannot count the number of times my train stopped at the station in Ostrów Wielkopolski. The name of the station was staring me in the face, yet my heart and mind had shut off all the history linking me to this place; and I continued on my way south.

One day, my business colleague who travelled with me on these trips got off in Łódź; I helped him with his luggage and watched him go. Quite tall, his once blond hair now turned mousy-grey, and at the age of well over seventy, his frame remained strong, upright, and masculine. But on that day, his shoulders sagged, his head drooped, the whole body somehow shrivelled as he walked towards the exit pulling his suitcase. I recall his words: *this is the platform from which I caught the last train out of Łódź… in 1940… my father had a textile factory in those buildings there…* Yes, he was a Jew, he told me so at our very first meeting, as if that was going to make any difference to our relationship – surely, it is the man that counts, his personality, not his religion or nationality… and he was a remarkable man.

My face saved my life. I was big and had wavy blond hair and blue eyes... Nazis would never have suspected... I was taken in and sheltered by a Polish volkesdeutsh family... And I recall his words when, one day, we were standing at the intersection of the streets by the old Prudential building in Warsaw: *the biggest challenge I faced at the time of the Warsaw Uprising was to run from one side of this street to the other... and survive Nazi bullets. That building there was a hospital... my father was in it... I had to come.*

And one day I, too, did get off the train and walk the three or four kilometres from the railway station in Ostrów Wielkopolski; I did enter that street, and I did knock on that door... *My name is Sławek...* Ula, having opened the door, looked at me with a blank expression on her face... *I am Sławek... from London... Kubica...* and that was all I could say, for tears rolled uncontrollably down my cheeks. I was sixty-six at that time – surely, not the age to cry; but they rolled. Ula was instantly electrified. *Mama, mama... come quick! Look who's come!*

Indeed the "Prodigal Son" had returned, not to the domain of his father for he had long since departed, but to his cousins, and to his father's hometown. And indeed, a welcome with open arms and a feast befitting the biblical Prodigal Son was laid on for me. But I was late – if only by a year – to embrace the last living member of my closest family, to hear first-hand about their life and the history of those that stayed behind in the town and the village of my father's birth.

And, at long last, I was ready to rendezvous with my father's, and my grandfather's history, and his birthplace in the nearby village of Wielowieś.

· · · · · · · · ·

…one hot summer day in the early 1920's a man stepped aside onto the dusty tract to let pass an oncoming chaise when he was suddenly stung by the tip of a whip on his face and neck. *Scum! Take off your hat when I am passing* – shouted the landlord. The man caught the hat as it fell off his head and held it clenched in his fist. His eyes gleamed – one day… one day…

· · · · · · · · ·

What had been blocking my heart and mind for so many years? Was it perhaps a chance remark I had heard at home in London that had subconsciously cut off for so many years all feelings of empathy for my relatives in Poland? Was it the mental picture those words conjured in my mind?

…"b*ród, smród i głód*" - I heard my father utter these words, to whom, and on what occasion, I don't remember, but I know in my soul that he was talking of his birthplace. I was a boy then, but those words remain embedded in my memory. Is this the reason why I had never visited Wielowieś? Never had the humility to visit my father's birthplace even though on many occasions, I was only some twenty kilometres distant from it?

Finally, at the age of 66, I overcame this spiritual barrier; I went to Wielowieś; I met my cousins… and my tears of shame flowed beyond my control.

…"*filth, stench and hunger*" - were these my father's

boyhood memories of Wielowieś? But his are tough people - big and strong of build, even stronger and tougher in spirit. Their welcoming embrace is like a bear-hug; you feel the hard work they had put into life; no-nonsense, nothing soft or particularly emotional about them; you sense determination, their strong character. They are *"Poznaniuki"* – people from the Poznań region, brought up in the mental and physical rigor of the Prussians, yet Poles to the core. My father was one of them, perhaps a little softer than most. So it's not surprising that after two hundred years of oppression, intimidation and Germanization, the Prussians still couldn't break their spirit - and they knew it. As a child I read with passion the story *"Wóz Grzemały"*, set at the time the Prussians forbade the Poles to build homes on their plot of land, so Grzemała built a house… on wheels. A caravan home!

My eldest two uncles were conscripted into the Prussian army in 1914 – they had no choice, they lived in Prussia. But the Prussians knew they could never trust them to fight in situations where their Polish brothers might face them on the opposing side. Stories abound of shouts *"nie strzelajcie my swoi!"* as Poles from the Prussian trenches tried to cross to their brothers on the opposing side… *"don't shoot, we are with you!"* Very few crossed safely.

And so it was with my two uncles. Their orders were to stop the first bullet, to be the battlefield fodder, to give Prussian soldiers a better chance… and both were killed – somewhere in Verdun, but exactly when, how, where - no one knows. Were they shot in the heart by their Polish brothers on the side of the Allies, or killed by a Prussian bullet in the back while attempting to cross the lines? But my grandmother knew her sons' destiny; she knew it in her heart; she felt it in her bones. Each day, I was told, she would walk out onto the field behind the house to pray, to weep and wait for the dreaded news... until she heard... and she too died of a shattered heart.

My father wanted to escape the *"filth, stench and hunger"* of his birthplace; he wanted better than this for his family and for Poland. His loyalty was forever to Poland. In 1918, still not quite eighteen then, he joined Powstanie Wielkopolskie (Uprising in Wielkopolska) and fought the Prussians, street by street, to liberate Poznań and the region. He fought them hand-to-hand, with sabre, with bayonet, eye to eye - your guts or mine! Then, at the age of 20, he fought in the Bolshevik war: in the glorious advance all the way to Kiev, in the shocking shambles of the Polish retreat from Kiev all the way back to the outskirts of Warsaw, and in the "miraculous" rout of the Bolshevik armies on the river Vistula – *"Cud nad Wisłą"*. He always fought for the creation of a new, independent Poland.

He rose again to fight the German invasion in 1939; he survived Stalin's GULAG, and lived to fight them again, under General Anders in Monte Casino and in Ancona. He was 47 before he could begin to hope for peace in his life... not in Poland, now under communist regime, but perhaps in the UK – a very high price to pay for the hope of a better life. In those previous 30 years he had, at best, just eight years of happy family life in Postawy, in the new-Poland of the 1920s.

Everyone in Poland knew in 1939 that war with Germany was imminent but hoped it would not come... not just yet... not today... please. So when the first bombs fell and the news of the war spread, panic in Wielowieś spread like wild fire. Carts and wagons were loaded with their owner's meagre possessions of food, bed sheets, eiderdowns, chickens, pigs, utensils, children, expectant mothers... their one cow hitched to the wagon and the whole miserable cavalcade rushed at cow's pace to... where? No one knew exactly where to go, which way to turn; one thought, one fear numbed their minds – get away from the front, away from the Germans... go east... hide in the woods... towards the bridge over the river Prosna in Raduchów... or in exactly the opposite direction over the bridge in the nearby Ołobok...

But they didn't trudge far or for long; the German war machine, like a blast of hot air had traversed the few kilometres from the German border to Wielowieś, and was way past the cavalcade. Babies were being born in the wagons... women, old men, children, cows... were all exhausted; there was no sense in what they were doing. Two cyclists rode up to the cavalcade shouting: *Hey, don't be stupid! Germans are saying we should stay on our land, live like normal, work like always, they won't hurt us...* And so the cavalcade turned back the next day. But life was not "like normal".

Helena, a friend of my cousins, was twelve years old at the time; she remembers those early days of German occupation. *When the war broke out, all our young men had already been called up and the Poznań Army went to fight in defence of Warsaw. Germans dropped leaflets onto the streets of*

Warsaw saying that all soldiers, who would lay down their arms and surrender, will be free to go home to work as normal. And, in fact, that's what happened. After the capitulation of Warsaw, our men came back by train to Ostrów and then walked home. Life was good then. We worked on our plots of land; we were never short of food. Of course, we had to give hefty contingents of food and crops to the Germans; all horses were taken by the Germans, all livestock listed; heavy penalties if you dared slaughter a pig - you were likely to be executed yourself. But we always found a way to get around this. We lived… much better than ever before in the years of Piłsudski regime - those were truly years of utter poverty and hunger.

Her son-in-law must have seen the surprise on my face. *My dear Sir, let me tell you straight how it was. Around here, the land was owned by the Graf - a very rich landlord. People worked for him on his land – for them it wasn't so bad. But all others tilled their little plot of land, perhaps had one cow, few chickens and little else… their life was one of "bród, głód i smród". When Piłsudski was here, life was awful. In a family I know, the husband worked as a train conductor – that was a very good job indeed, and they had money. His wife was persuaded to donate all their gold coin savings towards the Polish cause; a little later, he died in a train crash and his wife was left with five children and - nothing! No savings, no state compensation, no pension – she was destitute! She had to work wherever… in a brick factory… just to earn a pittance to save her five children. That's Poland for you! When the Russians came, they said they will leave soon… well, they didn't! But, at least, they brought and left some good here. They introduced the PGRs (State Farms), introduced better cultivation and husbandry methods, new farm machinery… Peasants learned from them, bought old farm machinery from the PGRs… At long last, peasant life started to improve!*

Helena continued: *Oh no, you couldn't build a house or anything else in those days without permission from the Germans. No one went to school - it was closed. When the Allied bombings of Germany started, they housed German youth in the school to keep them safe. There was a German administrator to look after them; they never mixed with us. And, of course, we had to give more to the Germans to keep this German youth well fed! But it was good life, in comparison with Piłsudski years.*

But not every man tilled his plot of land. Others, as partisans or saboteurs, continued to fight the German occupier. Gunfire was often heard in the local forests; traitors will always be found even amongst friends. One night a man knocked on the door of a house in *Ceglana* Street in Wielowieś. He carefully and persuasively explained his need to contact the local partisan group. The two men inside the house agreed to show him the way; they stepped outside and... straight into the hands of the Gestapo. They were led to the back of the house and shot dead on the spot.

And to think that it took 1,865 years to abolish serfdom in Europe; another 50 years and WW1 before the serf began to feel like a rightful human being, and still another 30 years and WW2 before the descendants of the same serf had the right and the means to fully participate in the life of the Nation – nay, even to lead the Nation.

And who would have foreseen in the 1920's that from amongst the third generation of this "scum" of Wielowieś, would come the doctors, teachers, physiotherapists, engineers, economists, accountants, agro-scientists, environmentalists, administrators... the same "scum", now saving lives of the descendants of the once landlords of Wielowieś; taking care of their well-being in homes for the aged in Poland, USA, England...

And who would have thought at that time that, in the year 2005, the same "scum" will become the good citizens and voters in the new society of the new Poland in the new Europe of the new - 21$^{st.}$ century?

But I was too late by three, two, even just one year... for by the year 2005, no one from amongst my relatives was still alive in Wielowieś or Ostrów who could fill in the missing pages of my father's life and history... those early years of poverty, struggle, sacrifice for his family and for Poland. So how can I explain it now if I don't understand it myself... why didn't I ask, why didn't I listen?

But, on September 1$^{st.}$ 1939, my father was not in Wielowieś; he was in the northeast, in Postawy, called up to fight the German threat...

But, one day he did return. I was living in a resettlement camp in England by then, when a man in khaki and black beret walked back into my life... eight years to the day almost, after that fateful day in September 1939. But where had he been all those eight years? How had these long years of absence shaped his life... his character? And who am I; who is this son of 'a man in khaki and a black beret'?

The return of the "Prodigal Son" provided only part

of the answer. I needed to know more, to understand more... I became overwhelmed with a sense of urgency to set out on a journey in search of his footprints, and the footprints of those hundreds of thousands other men like him, abandoned in the depths of Stalin's evil empire.

2

Into Oblivion

Mommy... where's daddy? Why isn't he here? Why has he gone away? Why can't we...?

But what could mother say - that the war had broken out, that dad left a week ago to fight the Germans? Who knows where he is now... alive, dead? She could only hug the little girl of seven closer... *shhh, shhh, everything will be all right... he will be back...* She knew she had to be strong for the sake of her three small children - one a baby of six months. She was soldier's wife, but she couldn't stop tears welling in her eyes, and they flowed quietly, pleadingly... *Oh Lord! Please let him come back safe.* Outside in Wileńska Street men with red armbands were marching people away... soldiers in long shabby coats, caps with blue bands, bayonets...

... ...

A little boy was tugging at his mother's coat at the railway station in Wilno. As people walked past, they slowed down...

Mommy, mommy, why are these men on their knees, why are they going up the ramp into those wagons? Mommy... who are those men with guns and red stars on their cap... why are they pushing them like that? Mommy...
Shush child... these are Russian soldiers pushing Polish men, Polish prisoners...

Hell! What if somewhere amongst those men on their knees... was my father.

....

Day 1... 2... day 3... and they are still cramming Polish men into wagons. But by now, Soviet guards had a better idea: the prisoners had to squat, put their hands behind their backs and hop - yes, hop - up the ramp into the wagons! And if you think that's funny - try it! And if you are not very good at it - don't worry; a blow, or two, from a rifle-butt about your kidneys should teach you the trick. And if it doesn't - don't worry. A few more rifle butts around your kidneys and your head will fix that - two men will eventually pick you up by your shoulders and dump your limp body onto the floor of a wagon.

And what if my father was one of these men? I shudder at the thought!

Eventually, the men with guns and red stars on their caps could squeeze no more men into the wagons at the railway station in Wilno. Doors slammed shut, keys grated in the padlocks, the barking of guards' dogs stopped, semidarkness engulfed the men inside the wagons, the train jerked, wheels started turning...

The euphoria of Poland's independence regained in 1920, the hope for better future, the smile on Polish faces – they were all gone now. It was bad enough facing German blitzkrieg but nobody foresaw the red "tsunami" that was to hit Poland on 17th. September,

1939; it came in the shape of the Red Army and the millions of its men, tanks and guns. Total bewilderment numbed men's minds: how could it have happened? Why? Where? Who's to blame... the government, the politicians, the generals? The bubble of more and more heated arguments rose: what about France and England - our Allies - and the promised help? After all, they all fought, as Poles had always done - *'Za Waszą Wolność i Naszą'*: 'For Your Freedom and Ours'. Remember Poniatowski? Remember Kosciuszko in the American War of Independence? Remember King Sobieski in the battle of Vienna? Who halted the Turks from annihilating Europe - if not the Poles? And who stopped Tatar hordes from annihilating Europe – if not the Poles?

You naïve people! Who fights for YOUR freedom? Don't you know? Will you never learn? Your freedom is a matter of political expediency, of national self-interest to others, of dollars, pounds, shillings and pence; never count on, or expect, anything more! Didn't you know that while your country was being engulfed by the German blitzkrieg from the west and the "red tsunami" from the east, your Allies were fighting the 'phoney war', as Churchill had put it himself? Will you never learn?

… … … …

Rat tat tat… rat tat tat... rat tat tat… No, no… it's not machinegun fire - too regular for that - it's the wheels of the train; and they go on and on and on…

Day one... two... three... who knows how many! Suddenly someone whispers - Moscow. The whisper erupts. People press towards the tiny window up above, peer through cracks in the timber walls of the wagon... they recognize the domes of Orthodox churches - Moscow! Ah... now they know!

And the wheels of the train go on and on and on drumming it into their heads: Si-ber-ia... Si-ber-ia... Si-ber-ia... for where else could it be? Whether it's the Tsar, or Lenin or Stalin... Siberia has always been there to welcome them, to swallow them all.

Siberia - the land of tears, pain and agony; land of exile and heart-breaking yearning for freedom and for their own beloved country. Siberia – the destination for how many hundreds of thousands of Polish freedom fighters, politicians, generals, soldiers, intellectuals, students, even peasants.

Who can forget the Kościuszko uprising against the Tsar in 1794, or the November uprising in 1830, or the third uprising against the Tsar in January 1863, and the partition of Poland between its historical foes: Russia, Prussia and the Austro-Hungarian Empire? And after each futile but heroic uprising, many thousands of Polish freedom fighters and sympathizers from all walks of life were executed, imprisoned or deported to Siberia. And now? A de-facto fourth partition of Poland between the same two foes - Russia and Germany ... and the world looked on and gave its stamp of acceptance. You heroic, naïve, cocky people - when will you learn!

A feeling of foreboding descends on the souls of the prisoners; hush… men cringe; shivers run up the spine and numb the brain. Suddenly, in this cramped space, a man stands to attention and from the depth of his chest and heart blares out the Polish National Anthem – *Jeszcze Polska nie zginęła póki my żyjemy*. Instantly, the wagon is electrified; the national anthem explodes; the sound carries and is picked up by men in other wagons. The entire train lives through a moment of national pride, hope and will. But how long can a song last? How long can it uplift men's moral when hunger begins to gnaw? When all you are given is a bowl of "piss-soup" - no, not pea-soup - a salty herring and 400gms. of stale bread. When men around you begin to die and cadavers are unceremoniously dumped by the rail tracks. But they all still ardently believe in the words of the National Anthem - "Poland lives on as long as we are alive".

… … …

Rat tat tat… rat tat tat… rat tat tat… No, no… it's not machinegun fire - not yet, not today… It's the wheels of their train still going on, and on, and on…

Eventually, the train stropped, locks grated, doors slid open, guard dogs bared their teeth…Get out! Out! Form into fives! And remember: one step to the left, one step to the right out of the column… and we shoot to kill!

And now… they have been trudging, through deep snow… for how many days? Who can tell in this country of permanent night in the winter months in the north of Russia? Those at the front found this death-walk toughest for they had to tread waist-deep in the virgin snow; those following them compressed the snow even further so that the last strugglers were walking on a man-made white tract. But that didn't help the strugglers much; there was no place for them in the column - guard dogs would bite at their shins, rip at their rags, until finally starving, exhausted, they would drop and stay - a frozen road marker along the way. Only their clothes, their rags, their meagre possessions would be stripped off and cherished; a bullet perhaps would spare them agony.

And that young Latvian - remember...? Yes, yes, the one you might have sat next to in the prison cell in Vilnius? A strong, young man - if anyone could, he would have survived; yet when his old father collapsed, he cradled him in his arms; he stayed... the dogs, the rifle butts, the kicks... yet he stayed! And the two gunshots you heard? You know what they meant. What would you have done... what would I have done?

Would I have stayed? Or would I have found compelling reasons to march on, to live on?

Far too exhausted, frozen, starving to look anywhere other than at their feet, the strugglers missed the first glimmer of some lights ahead, but the guards knew where they were and harassed the column to move faster. As they cleared the trees, a huge gateway just ahead of them loomed out of the darkness, flanked by a high watch tower with a machine gun and searchlight trained on them. Powerful searchlights further to the left and right of the gate periodically shook hands with the searchlight on the tower and lit up high barbed wire fencing extending into the distance. On the way from Moscow to here, wherever the "here" was, they had seen many such *lagiers*, but this one was different - this one was meant for THEM!

A foreboding gloom descended on the men. A 'haunted castle' was ready to suck them in - haunted by the near-dead, men such as they themselves were soon to become, and haunted by the NKVD as they were soon to discover.

The gateway doors swung open... five abreast, they staggered through the gate and into the holding compound inside. The NKVD guards counted them: five, five, five... and just a glance around the enclosure was enough to see that their number now was much smaller than the thousand that had set out on this trek. The high barbed wire fencing of the inner enclosure surrounded them...

- *Wait! Stand! Sit...* But still no food, still no drink...
- *Wait!* And so, they waited. A little further, lay the camp proper: long barracks virtually submerged in snow piled high, deep channels dug in snow ran between the barracks and other points of the camp.

The camp's Procurator climbs onto the podium; men stand to attention.

Listen!
   - *Rule number 1 - you don't work; you don't eat.*
   - *Rule number 2 - when marching in a column, remember:*

> *one step to the left, one step to the right - the guards will shoot to kill.*
> - *Rule number 3 – mind the death zones. Ten meters inside the barbed wire fencing - step into it - guards shoot to kill.*
> - *And you can add rule number 4 - there is no escape from here; if the guards don't kill you, you will perish in the taiga!*
> - *Any questions..? Yes? Go ahead... you, you and you...*

Brave, but still "uneducated", voices speak up: *We haven't had any food or drink for the past two days; we are starving... our feet, our hands and face are severely frost bitten; we need some clothing, we are in rags...* The Procurator listens attentively, only the faintest semblance of a 'smile' flickers around his lips; he takes no notes – he has good memory. Or has he heard it all so many times before? But he promises to pass all the grievances to the camp commandant.

The men didn't have to wait long for his response.

As the Commandant rushes onto the podium, short, squat - a bull with horns hidden under his flat-roofed cap - seething with rage, face crimson, the men stand transfixed...

> - *You scum... you sobs... you mfcs... you think the procurator will help you! You dare complain! You dare demand! I am the master of your life and death here – you mfcs! When you leave the gate and walk in a column to your place of work... who do you think is master then!? It's my armed guards, you stupid sobs! They can kill you, maim you, give to their dogs... kick you to*

> *death… and what can your procurator do? F-all! Remember that!* – and he whips out his pistol.
> - *Line them up!* And they all line up.
> - *Every tenth man step forward!* Who would want to step forward with the man in this mood, but the guards force every tenth man forward.
> - *Take them out!*

The guards march the group out the way they had entered, through the huge gate, and into the beyond… How many? One hundred? More? There was no pretence; no hiding the horror, the enormity of it all… they all heard machine gun fire… and then a few single shots… No doubt left in their minds now. Crystal clear! Dead cert!

Thank God my father wasn't one of the every-tenth-man; he survived, he lived through it all. Thank God? How dare I say; how dare I even think in terms of "thank God"! My father lived on to save his wife and children, his closest family – five, perhaps ten people in all. But what about the one hundred or more every-tenth-man; what about the tragedy in their families – do we say "thank God" for that too? What convoluted explanations of God's will must we concoct to assuage the pain inside the families of those 'one hundred' men?

But where was this place, this "HERE" for my father? Was it the prison of Pavliszchev Bor or Kozielsk, or Vologda, or Kotlas, or some other transitory camp for the thousands of prisoners? Whichever one it was, he would not have been kept there for long; the omnipotent, omnipresent NKVD would have already prescribed his fate and sent him on an *etap* – on a journey - to his... end.

He didn't talk much of those years, but some fragments of talk at home resurface from the depths of my memory - Murmansk... Kola Peninsula... Archangelsk... Alas, who still lives to tell the story first-hand?

But follow their footprints, and the story of their years in "Stalin's Evil Empire" will unfold, slowly, reluctantly.

Just a day, or so, before 1st September, 1939, my father left Postawy, his home and his family, and moved with groups of other policemen and border guards towards Wilno where they were all to join up with Polish regular troops in the region. But within the first few days of the war, Polish armies in the northeast of Poland were routed by the German blitzkrieg and he would have had no choice but to cross the border into neutral Lithuania. There, he would have been interned in a camp, possibly in Rokiszki.

Then came September, 17th 1939 - the day the Red Army crossed the Polish border, the day the fate of Poland was sealed between Stalin and Hitler; it was the day my father's fate was sealed also.

At that time, Lithuania was independent and neutral, but not for long. In June 1940 Lithuania became part of the USSR and the Soviets took over the internment camps. The NKVD was ready; the fate of the internees was approved and sealed beforehand. In the next day or so, some 2000 Polish internees were transported to more secure prisons in Kozielsk. From there, Polish officers were sent to an even more secure prison - to their death in Katyn.

But my father, a non-commissioned policeman, would have been spared that fate – Stalin had plans for his muscle, though not his soul. His life was now entirely expendable, but while he was still alive.... cattle wagons were ready to take him and thousands other prisoners like him north to work in the Workuta coalmines, lay rail tracks in the Uhta GULAG, build roads and lay rail tracks on the Kola Peninsula, or work on military installations along the coastline of the Barents Sea, or cut lumber in the limitless taiga... Stalin's choice, his practicality and ingenuity were limitless; human life was expendable in Stalin's Grand Plan.

I can only wonder what that little boy from Wilno would have seen at the railway station in Kozielsk or at any of the other transfer stations, for these men were all condemned now. They were no longer internees in a neutral country, not even prisoners of war - for, ironically, the Soviets entered Poland as the country's "liberators", to give it an "appropriate" government; Stalin was not at war with Poland!

My father and others like him became common criminals now, or worse: accused of treason, they became condemned men. Can you imagine Polish soldiers fighting Hitler, taken over as internees by the Soviet army in the annexed Lithuania, and then accused of treason against - Russia! And the penalty: death by immediate execution, or to be worked to death in GULAG *lagiers*.

Indeed, where was my father in those years of War. Why didn't I ask while he was still with us… didn't I listen, or didn't he say? How can we not know the history of those tragic years; how can we not pass it on to our children and their children?

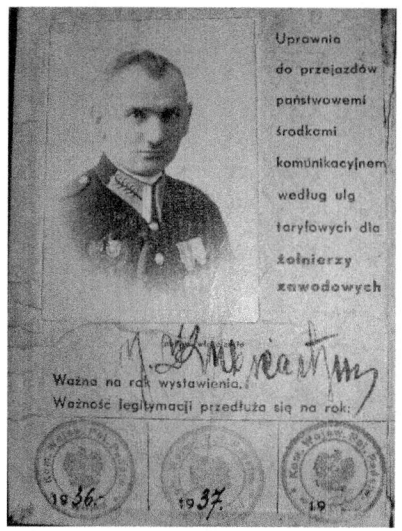

My father, Postawy - 1937

In the Anders Army - August 1942

Attestation – father's participation in Wielkopolskie Uprising of 1918 – he was just 18 at the time.

My father's Monte Cassino Cross 1945

My father's birthplace in Wielowieś - 2010

Our home in Postawy - 2010

3

Footprints in Russia

Ask a man deported to Siberia - you get one answer;
Ask any Communist Party Member - you get another.
Ask a man executed for his views - you get... silence,
The safest option practised in "Stalin's Evil Empire".

… … …

At thirty five thousand feet up in the air, a pink tinge appeared on the horizon to my right. It was expanding perceptibly; delicate, soft colours turning deeper and richer began to envelop the plane. I was mesmerised. The noise of the engines, the lights, the passengers didn't exist; I was being caressed by the most delicate ostrich feathers in delicate pinks. This metamorphosis of the sky continued into deeper, richer, denser, pinks; I was floating somewhere deep inside a heavenly marshmallow, at peace with all, detached from all, perhaps buried somewhere in the bosom of angels.

Was this heaven then? The colours of this heavenly environment deepened into richer reds transiting into violets, then transiting quickly into deeper, darker, ominous shades. But my state of total oblivion persisted and I must have closed my eyes for a moment or two; when I opened them next, I was shocked to find myself being rapidly enveloped by a black *purga*. I have read and heard of white *purga* in Siberia and the Arctic, of total whiteout, of howling winds and snow, of total loss of spatial orientation, of sure death to anyone who ventures out while it rages, and now I was in its black equivalent! If this is Hell - I was in it!

A little later, I could see lights way below me, inviting, ready for me... Hell! I had a glimpse of what heaven could be and I was brutally expelled from it; I was being taken back to Earth - to hell, to Mankind... and I stepped out onto the land of the GULAG through the gateway Leningrad.

... ...

Workuta, Abez, Inta, Pechora, Uhta... Arkhangelsk, Murmansk... the venues for the "end game" played out in GULAG *lagiers*. NKVD set the rules, and they were stacked against you; the stakes were high – lives, your life too.

If you had the physical strength and mental resilience, you might have lasted a month, a year, five, ten, or even longer, in *a lagier* but if you could play out the game to the mid-1950's you might well have won and found yourself going home, or have become a "free" man on a six-kilometre leash... if not, you lost - your life.

The fore-game was much shorter but even more destructive: a brutal mental and physical torture - a month, a year, perhaps three in the cells and interrogation rooms of NKVD prisons in Wilno, or Lwów, or Białystok, then Moscow or Kharkov, or in other prisons only known to them. They would call you out at night, over and over again; no sleep, beatings, threats and questions, questions and questions: give us names, names and names – your name… that of your friends, colleagues, associates in your subversive activities. You have become an enemy of the people, anti-Communist, anti-Soviet and finally, in their eyes, you have become a traitor!

Admit! Admit! Sign here!

Admit your guilt and you live… to die in a *lagier* repenting for sins you never committed, or you die now!

What? You won't admit, you won't sign? No?

And… as the blood streams from your face, your legs give under you, the faces of your family eddy in your mind, you blank out…

You barely hear the judge pronounce the verdict – Section 58! You know the penalty – execution! You have no lawyers, no media to take up your cause, no Amnesty International… you are not even on the map of the living; what chance do you have? So you wait in the death cell, and wait, and wait, and wait… your turn.

But what do I know of what goes on in the mind of a man held in a death cell awaiting execution? Our fathers and grandfathers knew; my father wouldn't speak of it, many others seize up at the mention of it.

Some still remember… You rot for days in a death-cell, a subterranean pit, damp, cold; the spy-hole is the only source of light when it opens. You are alone, your mind swings wildly from thoughts about your dear ones to a state of bottomless depression, for you know your future, the question is only – when? With sheer willpower, you muster a semblance of calmness, of rationality but just then... you hear muffled shots in the night. Now... you hear boots stamping in the corridor... the steps are getting closer, and closer, and closer... your hair rises, you cringe like a dog fearing a kick... and they don't stop! They pass your cell! Thank God... not me, not tonight! And you sink to the floor exhausted by the sudden relief that it's not you, not tonight, not yet... Then you hear them again... nearer and nearer... and this time they stop at the door to your cell! Keys jingle and grate in the lock... door opens! They have come... it must be that they have come for you... for there's nobody else in the cell... it's your turn... You don't have the strength to get up; the guard pulls you up... and you hear: get up!

Get up! Take your things!

What! Did you hear right? Take your things? *Take your things...take your things... take...* reverberates in your mind. So it's not to be - no execution, not just yet, for if they were going to shoot you now, they would have said - leave your things... and fresh hope flashes in your mind.

And you are led away in the middle of the night under escort, dumped into a truck, and then unloaded into wagons waiting for you at rail sidings. You are oblivious of the snow, wind and freezing cold penetrating you to the bone, for your death sentence has been commuted! You live! You are still healthy enough, strong and resilient enough to work for the glory of the Soviets, to spend the next five, ten, fifteen years or more in a GULAG *lagier*; that's a more profitable way for Stalin to dispose of you.

The wagon jerks, the wheels begin to turn… Moscow, Vologda, Kotlas… One week, two, three… and the wheels still turn, but there are moments when you forget your misery, your hunger, thirst and absolute exhaustion. Casually, you look up at the sky through the bars in the windows of the *Stolypin* wagon and you are stunned by the beauty of the mass of diamonds sparkling in the deep black sky. The Northern Star, like a magnet, pulls the train north, further and further north; distances extend into infinity, the night extends into infinity… and the further north you go, the brighter they sparkle. But that awe-inspiring beauty exists only there - in the heavens; suddenly you become painfully aware that you are still on earth, and still a prisoner.

The train slows down to walking pace. The white walls of snow piled high along the rail tracks are ready to engulf you; temperature of -40°C is ready to freeze you, yet there in the clearing, a group of men stand aside to let the train pass. Covered in rugs beyond recognition, some stand aimlessly, others rest on their tools or huddle by the raging bonfire; they return your look with unseeing, uncomprehending eyes… For them it's a brief moment of respite; for you, it's a live snapshot of what awaits you. A little further, the train stops – is it your turn? Is it Uhta, Inga, Abez, Pechora, Workuta or Arkhangelsk perhaps? They won't even tell you.

Rat tat tat… rat tat tat… rat tat tat… No, no… it's not machinegun fire, not now… It's the wheels of a train… my train… going on and on, and on taking me to Workuta.

Stolypin wagons and steam engines have long gone from Russian railways but the rail tracks heading north are as endless as those in the winter months of the 1940's, only the snow has gone and those sparkling diamonds in the sky have gone too, for days are endless in mid June 2011. I am following in the footsteps of the thousands of prisoners - Russian, Polish, Ukrainian, and of many other nationalities – taken north to build this railway line and to fell trees in the endless taiga.

Day one, two, three… and the train still rolls along the green toboggan route. Trees, trees and trees line the track on both sides of the rails; what's hidden behind them is hard to tell – boundless taiga or open plains? At times one can almost feel the impenetrable density of fir, pine and birch, but only a little further up the track, the sun shines through the trees and heats the wagon to discomfort. Gradually, imperceptibly, the world changes – claustrophobia eases, rivers cross our way, water-logged terrain creates illusions of lakes, trees become smaller, sparser - dwarves in comparison with the proud firs earlier along the route… the terrain expands into a wide, expansive, barren horizon. Nothing to excite, nothing to shock or entertain the eye or mind… if only Russia wasn't so huge, if only distances weren't so huge, if only this train would move faster… How boring, boring and dull, lifeless…

Boring? Now I know what was bothering me, what was so painful, depressing... All the way north of Kozhva, the rail tracks follow a line of crosses, some still upright, others prostrate on the ground, or at odd angles, or totally overgrown by birch, or with their feet rotting in swampy terrain... Yet another veritable "Via Calvarias" of the Soviet era! A cross every fifty metres, some still linked by copper wires strung on the arms; dead bodies have been taken off, buried somewhere along the track or dumped in the swamps, but bits of porcelain, like bone, stayed attached...

Ah, now it's easy to put two-and-two together; now it's obvious why in an open and barren terrain that particular copse of birch stands strong, erect, its bark perfectly white in the sun; or why that or that cross still stands upright, firmly held by strong and healthy clumps of trees. True, these "crosses" were poles put up by prisoners to carry telephone and electricity wires, but is that important? It's common knowledge today that thousands of prisoners died along these railway tracks - one life for every pole - more or less - who would have counted or worried about such numbers back in the 1940's? Who would bother burying the dead in cemeteries? A common grave or pit here... another there... and there... and so the birch trees grow white and strong... here... and there... and there...

Lifeless? As if to prove me wrong, the view from the carriage window startles me, brings a smile to my face, makes me wonder what century I am living in. There is life here, after all, even in this forgotten outback. Two women in colourful attire squatting by a running stream launder clothes on a boulder and look at the passing train with equal surprise. And... here's a dwelling almost on top of the tracks - a lean brownish pig rummages in the front garden while a dog looks unperturbed by the passing train; a chicken scurries away in fright; a small child crawls happily in their midst... A little further along the track a shirtless man fills two large buckets from a standpipe in the street and staggers with them back to his abode... And again, there... a station administrator with a lollipop in her hand stands to attention as the train pulls away, her face solemn, eyes rigidly focused on some point beyond this world, mind focused on her pension, her job... or perhaps mercifully - blank, oblivious to the anachronism of her job.

But in between these touching snapshots from the Soviet era, industrial and social dinosaurs lie dead along the tracks brought down by the Capitalist disease from the West in the early 1990's. Cadavers of massive industrial plants, eyeballs gouged out, teeth pulled or smashed, skin covered in leprosy, their flesh now rots in the Russian climate. Or those long barracks of an agricultural *kolkhoz* like the skull of a prehistoric man, low and heavy brow over a row of empty eye sockets... the maggots have been led out to be fattened, then eaten. Or that impressive residence labelled "Dwor" on the portico - it could well have been a Manor House of one of the Polish gentry - now abandoned and crumbling, eyes gaping open, mouth contorted in a grimace, slates like dandruff falling off its roof... all left in place to show Communism's contempt for the Gentry, or perhaps simply missed in the heat of the bloody Revolution.

How can it be boring? The moment my eyelids start drooping, I am again startled by the view from the window - there, quite plainly, hundreds of white masts appear on a large lake just ahead. Why here, in the outback of nowhere? Sailing boats? It can't be... surely not... every single hull is under water as if a tempest had flooded and sunk them all leaving only the masts still upright as their marker. The train rolls past... and the dead and bare, perfectly white trunks of silver birch stand rigid in the brown pool as they must have stood for years... perhaps even in the 1940's. As I open my eyes again later, I emerge into "nothing" - tundra: open, flat, cut by rivers, lakes, swampy terrain... limitless and boring. Boring? Try crossing it then; battle the mosquitoes and mites in summer, pull your boots out of the swamps... and if that's not enough of a challenge, challenge the white *purga* in winter!

The taiga continues seemingly into infinity, but eventually, this train, my train, will pull into a station, my station - Workuta. How many thousands of prisoners, perhaps my father among them, were pulled into this station? For so many, it was to be the end station... for it was where they were to play out their end-game.

Workuta (Vorkuta)

Workuta! One of the blackest and biggest warts on Mankind! Well beyond the Arctic Circle at 67° latitude north, set in bleak and barren tundra where only carbuncles made by man challenge the skies - slag heaps, like monumental molehills thrown up by tens of thousands of human moles burrowing the coal seams. In the land of the white *purga*, with temperatures as low as -50°C in winter and +30°C in summer, where the sun never sets during its two months of summer, and never rises during its long winters, the land of black coal, coal mines, *lagiers,* prisoners, pain and death... **Work-u-t-a**! The acronym for "**Work you to annihilation**".

Close my eyes... and I am instantly enveloped in whiteness; I cringe and shiver from bitter cold, walk bent double against the howling wind along narrow channels gouged deep in snow from one camp barrack to another, hold onto a guide-rope to lead me to the entrance of the canteen, or the hospital, give not a thought to that pile of cadavers frozen stiff under a cover of snow... And if I let my imagination blossom, the Nenets, or Komi people are here too, their herds of reindeer, tepees, children, men, women all a bundle of furs. All is hazy, enveloped in total or semi-darkness as if viewed through a soot-covered glass.

Close my eyes... and an old slide projector instantly flickers into life. Photographs from the album "GULAG – Life and Death inside the Soviet Concentration Camps" compiled by Tomasz Kizny pop up and reluctantly turn from one to the next. Workuta looms big and black, set in a hazy white background as in a poorly-focused black and white photograph; try to flick off the specs of red, and you can't... they are part of the setting. The slagheaps are the hallmark; at their feet lie the coalmines, the maze of railway tracks and... the *lagiers*! The watch towers stare back at me, the barbed wire encloses me; the mass of barracks overwhelms and testifies to the huge number of prisoners – 2000, 10000, 20000, 60000! And all embedded in what was once pure white snow now churned into ugly, wet, black, frozen mush. Wherever I look, and beyond the reach of my eyes - a slagheap, a mine, a camp, rail tracks, all fading into the distance. Workuta - the eye of an octopus, its tentacles, each with a mine for its sucker, reach out thirty kilometres.

Next, the photos from "Kręg Workuta" by Bernard Grzywacz, come to life. The slag heaps, the acres and acres of barracks set in barbed wire enclosures, the ubiquitous *wyshka*, the three-legged electricity distribution poles as if soldiers from outer space come down to earth to bestow power on the NKVD - all in the shabby-brown colour of fascism contrasting sharply with the purity of snow where it had not yet been touched by human foot or hand. A town built by the prisoners, for the prisoners, presided over by the watchful and brutal eye of the NKVD. The immensity of this place is staggering: the Kapitalnaya - mine #1 and its *lagier* for 6,000 prisoners; mine #9/10 and *lagier* for 10,000 prisoners!

… and then, the brick kilns in "Moje Powojenne Łagry" by Teresa Pawłowska. The furnace in the shape of a dome so hot inside that the pile of bricks stacked in it glows translucent red and… a team of six women, mottled in layers and layers of clothes, knock down the bricked-up access openings, rush in, shovel aside red-hot coals to get at the incandescent bricks… load them onto a trolley and pull the lot out

– by hand! Imagine… by hand! They have three and half minutes - three and half minutes of burning hell… any longer and they themselves burn in it! Facial hair singed, hands covered in heat blisters, the whole body burning hot; they rush out, drink litres of water from a barrel, throw themselves onto the snow, mud or whatever is wet, to get rid of the heat inside them… How long could one survive? How long before one goes crazy? Some survived a month! **Work…u…t…a**!

… and then this! It's unbelievable, so incongruous! The prison guards… posing, smiling for the camera! The NKVD bosses sitting in family circles; the prisoners engaging in intellectual pursuits in the library, in the common room, or the theatre; the prisoners ice skating, enjoying the spring, the flowers, the sunshine… couples getting married! But, of course, these photos were taken later, after the 1948 strikes, after Stalin's death, after the 1953 strikes, after 1956 when the hope of release and freedom and return to their homeland lit up prisoners hearts and faces.

And the "black" in the lives of men, so dramatically illustrated in the photographs from Margarita's private album. I will never forget: the "black" of the coal mines as they were in 1946, the "black" of the trains embedded in pristine snow, or the expedition into the northern abyss, or the indigenous Nenets with herds of reindeer… and everything suspended in grey opaqueness.

And as I step out of my train onto this wart one

Sunday early in June, I instantly "freeze" from the heat! 24°C! The sun beats down on me, dust bites into my eyes – where am I? What of the snow, the blizzards, the *purga* of the Arctic?

A bus takes me into town; a pinhead on a massive blue globe placed at crossroads announces: Workuta, 67° latitude north. The bus trundles on... past some rail tracks here, there, and there - some lead to nowhere, others to mines already dead and buried, no trains, no whistles, no lights at the crossings. Then across Metalovcy Square, dedicated to metal bashers, and the bus turns down Moskovskaya Street, the shopping and finance centre, and passes a magnificent façade of what was the theatre, the intellectual centre of the *lagier*-town, and down the long, wide road lined with shops and non-descript buildings on both sides. There is nothing extraordinary about this town - no barracks, no huge red stars mounted on buildings, or monuments to Stalin or Lenin; the origin and history of this town is not flaunted in your eyes - a "normal" town you might think... and there's my Hotel Vorkuta!

The attempt by Soviets to impress the proletariat by the size and magnificence of Soviet architecture remains in place – a dry fountain stands in the shaded approach to the huge hotel. A group of youths, already full of spirits by noontime, lounge at its foot, a mass of empty bottles and broken glass lay scattered on the pavement around it; will you dare walk past this architectural "jewel" at night?

Mine #8? I ask a pedestrian - *Just turn left as you exit the hotel, left again, walk down to the end, follow the promenade till you come to the monument... it's there, across the river.* So I walk... street after street of residential blocks - five storeys, seven storeys high, all almost identical, grey, drab concrete, facia peeling off. They were built on stilts to prevent the building sinking into the permafrost but that ventilation space has now been bricked up to keep away vandalism and drug abuse.

All the way down the slope to the river entire families and groups of people stripped naked to the minimum are picnicking, grills burning, obviously enjoying this moment. On the promenade by the river, groups of youths drink beer, sing, yet it's peaceful, relaxed... *Oh yes, we have work... in the mines...* a young man assures me with an obvious lack of conviction. Is this **Work-u-t-a**? Am I really north of the Arctic Circle? Not quite the south of France, not quite rural England here... but 24°C the first week of June?

On my side of the promenade lies the new Workuta: a maze of blocks dating to the nineties – dense and congested – so it's not surprising that its inhabitants seek relaxation on the green banks of the Workuta River, or congregate on the promenade, or just sit and gaze at their own recent history. Two elderly women sitting on a concrete block gaze wistfully to the far side of the river... *yes, we are local, we used to live just across, in that large block... now we all live here; the other place wasn't safe... no we don't remember the GULAG years...*

I too look across the river for the hallmarks of Workuta as they are embedded in my mind – the slag heaps, the mines, the maze of barracks, watch towers and barbed wire... Rudnik #8 has vanished, and so has its history - no slag heaps anywhere on the horizon, no barracks, no barbed wire, not a single *wyshka* in sight, no hint of its dreadful origins and its past. Only the cadavers of the Rudnik as it was in the 1990's face me from across the river. A massive residential block that was to be the pride of the new Rudnik - now its eyes gouged out let daylight pass right through its skull, its teeth pulled, brows singed, it stares at me and the people on the promenade... and they stare back - wistfully.

A little higher up, a magnificent façade of the administration building surveys its decayed dominion, itself taken from the pages of Greek history, it now crumbles in front of my eyes. Here and there other cadavers discretely covered by shrubs or grass protrude from the ground, and further out, on the crest of the raised terrain stand the remnants of the now-dead *Kapitalnaya* mine – the one million tons per year pride of Workuta. No trace of mines 2, 3...6... that once "adorned" the terrain opposite. Only the municipal thermal station is still alive and proudly belches volumes of smoke as black as the coal that feeds it. Beyond the borders of the Rudnik far to my right, the angular shapes of Vorkutinskaya mine cut sharply through the haze.

A young man and his girl walk me across the suspension bridge on the Workuta River. In the 1940's and 1950's this bridge was the Rubicon... cross it, and you leave your life in *Rudnik*. Crossing it to-day is hair-raising too: if you walk on legs – you will break them; if you wear loose shoes – you will lose them; if you are slim enough – you will slip through the gaps; if you think of safety – you wouldn't put your foot on it. Evidently, Workuta wants to keep you off it and out of *Rudnik*. Yet people, young and old, stream across it, for that's where they were born, where they lived, went to school, had better life there than they have now... for then, there was work, community, camaraderie... and now?

We walk among the cadavers of Rudnik; everything that's man-made crumbles – the buildings, roads and pavements, peoples' memories. *This was my school; that was the hospital, the canteen... Here stands what's left of the very first monument... there's a small graveyard for the geologists who lived, worked and died here... That white monument in the shape of a cross or open arms is for the Poles who worked and died here... if you follow the railway tracks for about half-hour you will find Polish graves in a neglected cemetery on the embankment... And here, right on the river bank was the entrance to the first mine...* now a crevice in the river bank overgrown with vegetation.

We are not alone here, quite a few other people walk through this history; youths congregate in small groups, bottles and broken glass at their feet but no rowdiness, no swearing. It's almost un-natural... are they doped by drugs or just good kids?

Where am I, I ask myself subconsciously again and again? Sunday, June 5, 11 pm, 24°C in the open, the sun still shines, only the cloudless sky appears grey and humourless and lacks clarity. People sit under marquees drinking beer, ordering shashlyk; provocatively dressed teenage girls act to catch the eye of youths, people parade along the main street... This? Workuta? North of the Arctic Circle? Really?

The defunct Kapitalnaya mine, once the pride of Soviet enterprise – one million tonnes of coal annually - now stands in isolation. It's easy enough to drive up the disintegrating concrete avenue leading to the mine and slip in through the main gate - no guards and no life here now. Its buildings stand empty but still carry their blue nametags: 1/3 Stancyonarnaya Ul. Above the entrance to the imposing main building, a mural shows a miner, drill in hand, at work at the coalface, and below him, at the side of the main entrance the blue plate announces: Lung Tuberculosis Clinic. Its door is flung fully open - no queues here, not now... but people in the train and around me in the streets still cough that deep worrying cough of TB.

The rear of the mine complex looks out onto open terrain – yes, now it's an open vista but barren and bleak and criss-crossed by tracks. A tall, slim metal tower bedecked with Soviet emblems: hammer & sickle, blazing red star, laurels of sheaves of wheat - still welcomes all who will come, but no one does. Well... I came, but not so many years ago, many were forced to come. This open foreground was fenced in, barb-wired in, congested with barracks, watched over by the *wyshka* and machineguns; columns of prisoners filed past the guardhouse and into the bowels of the mine. And if you look, you will still see stumps of the perimeter fence and strands of barbed wire at your feet; the cadaver of the guardhouse still bars your way – a shocking subject for "autopsy".

But it's Monday morning now, and the weather has flipped overnight from 24°C to just 4°C, and tomorrow's forecast is -4°C! All memories of the midnight sun, of beer and shashlyk under marquees, short sleeves and promenading youth... have been wiped out by the drizzle and penetrating cold. That "Monday morning feeling" we speak of on the way to work in London... what a painful joke in comparison with what the army of workers must have felt passing this spot just fifty years ago.

Mr Gorbachov what have you done! Now... *capitalist economics rule in Workuta. Before you, 250,000 lived here - now 85,000! Before you 20, 30, 40 mines operated here - now seven! The buildings you constructed crumble in front of our eyes. True... you have given us Glasnost so we can speak about it, but we can't live off it, can't eat it! Yeltsin gave away our wealth to the Mafia, but you, you have ruined our lives...* I have heard this many times before.

Glasnost – it's so easy. Put up a monument, put up two, three... like the one in the elbow of the promenade dedicated to the memory of those that perished in the *lagiers* of Workuta, or the monument across the river dedicated to the memory of Polish political prisoners, or the one where the leaders of the 1953 strike were executed... and you can now relegate the sixty years of Soviet labour camps and the GULAG to history! It's no longer "us"; we could be talking about Genghis Khan... The slag heaps have been levelled - the slag put back into defunct mines and into road surfacing; barbed wire removed, fencing removed, barracks knocked down and removed. Soon the incriminating cadavers will be buried too. The place where the brickworks stood could well be marked on the map now as a place of outstanding beauty with a magnificent view over the surrounding land of the once-GULAG. People may well soon ask - labour camps, GULAG, NKVD, unmarked burial grounds… really, where, when? And who will know if no one from the "Memorial" Foundation will be there to tell.

Of course, there is much more to Workuta than met my eye. There are statistics, cemeteries and burial grounds that I have not seen, but what I saw was enough! Mention Workuta to me and the slide projector instantly flickers into life again… No! No!

… … …

Rat tat tat… rat tat tat… rat tat tat… No, no… it's not machinegun fire - not today… it's the wheels of a train… my train… taking me deeper into the abyss.

Abez (Abis)

Strange… it's not easy to get to Abez today, yet in the 40's, thousands of people were arriving here daily. My only chance of getting to Abez is on the 05.00 hrs workmen's train from Workuta to Inta - if they will take me, for officially no passengers are allowed. The conductress is the boss on the train, takes 200 roubles off me and welcomes me on board.

Five hours later and some 200km. down the line the train slows down to a stop...

It's hard to imagine that any train would want to stop here, but the conductress is adamant - *yes, yes... this is where you get off... yes, this is Abez*! There's nothing here but one long concrete block for a platform along the rails and I can't even see the name of this place. Two or three workmen get off the train and quickly disappear. On the other side of the rails three or four motorbikes with sidecars roar in, pull up, churn the ground, and go away – local taxis, but no takers. I am left standing alone.

A few yards beyond the rail track a boardwalk leads to some buildings in the distance. I plod the half-kilometre cautiously for the spring mire has not yet quite dried out and the "catwalk" is unstable; a tall military communication tower on my left, several three-storey brick barracks, more motor bikes ploughing unpaved pathways, adolescents eyeing me with curiosity...

Is this Abez... "the" Abez... "the" centre of the ABEZ group of *lagiers* that had sent fear into the soul of prisoners throughout the entire GULAG system in the Komi Republic? Where, in the summer of 1938, 20,000 prisoners were brought in to work on railroad construction, and only two years later, less than 4,000 were still alive? Where the prisoner death rate was so high that even Stalin was shocked; and when the railway was done, he had the camp bosses put on trial for the high mortality amongst prisoners! The executioners of only yesterday were themselves sentenced to 10, even 15 years imprisonment?

A woman striding purposefully in my direction assures me: *yes, yes... this is Abez. Victor is the schoolteacher, just there, in that building, he's the historian. You can leave your rucksack in my shop, it's O.K...* I am happy to take up her offer for I have been told in Workuta that there is nothing to buy in Abez, so my rucksack is heavy with food and water.

Victor was born and bred in Abez, and now at the age of sixty, in 2011, he is retiring - the only teacher at the village school. Ever since "Glasnost" came in with Gorbachev, he dedicated his life, time and physical effort to the preservation of the history of GULAG camps in and around Abez. With perseverance and help from the "Memorial" Foundation, he succeeded in obtaining NKVD lists of persons buried in three cemeteries around Abez, and was then able to correlate the numbers on the graves with names and dates. Slowly, painstakingly, and almost single-handedly, he transformed the largest cemetery from one buried and forgotten in the shrubbery to one worthy of the memory of those buried here; now 1,296 graves have nameplates, not just numbers as if attached to the toe of a cadaver. And now, people can, and do come here, to pray, or meditate, or write the history of the generals, the bishops or the ordinary "enemies of the people" buried here. Thirteen more cemeteries lie along the railway line between here and Workuta but who can find them now when all documentation is buried deep somewhere in KGB files.

Damn these mosquitoes. There were none on the way up to Workuta, none on the way down, and hardly any in Abez itself, but right here... Victor is just a step or two ahead walking me around the cemetery. I can see mosquitoes landing on the bald-patch of his head, on his neck and shoulders, but they don't seem to bother him and, only now and then, he just swipes them away; but they love my sweet blood, and I hate every one of them.

Victor explains that mosquitoes suddenly appear with the first green shoots; and the cemetery is normally the first to "bloom". Is it not perhaps that, even after some 60-70 years, the abundant new growth, and the mosquitoes, still live off the nourishment under the posts with number plates... for Abez is in the region of permafrost and the graves would have been dug shallow. 1,296 numbered graves around me and two smaller cemeteries nearby... all in the neighbourhood of a settlement of only 750 people!

A strange fellow appears as if from nowhere and tags along for a while saying nothing, an empty sack slung over his shoulder, his distinctly Japanese features contrast incongruously with his white complexion – a descendant of Japanese prisoners, perhaps? We came across him again later, his sack was already partly full; his crime obvious: he was skimming the lichen off the cemetery grounds leaving ugly eczema on the surface that will take time to recover. Angry, Victor sent him off packing; his anger at the man is not surprising for, you could say, the cemetery is "his" – after twenty years dedicated to the preservation of the history of this place.

On the way back to the village we pass several barracks dating to the 1930-40's lying along what must have been the main road – *Polyarnaya 1… Polyarnaya 6…* Victor points to the ramshackle barrack he and his family had lived in until 1990 and, even now, people live in it. In those early days Abez was a thriving town built on the foundation of forced labour; it had shops, communal refectory, baths, social amenities including a theatre, well maintained tracks and, of course, the ubiquitous *tiurma* - the prison - the largest building in any town. By 1948, the Kozhva-Workuta railway was fully operational and Abez lost its pre-eminent status as the centre for railway construction, its population dwindled to 6,000 but the *lagier* remained. By 1958 most of the facilities were dismantled, the *lagier* closed down and any remaining prisoners transferred to other GULAG camps.

Over the years, Victor assembled an important collection of memorabilia from the Abez camps. Eventually, it became much too large to display in its entirety at the school so the Museum in Inta offered to take them and undertook to display the entire collection in an appropriate setting; naturally, Victor was delighted and signed his collection over to the museum. The Museum took the collection some five years ago and… nothing! Where is it, who has it, it's hard to know. Now Victor keeps the remainder of his collection safely under lock and key in two large metal containers rarely open to view by the public. Next to them, stand more recent housing blocks. They were hastily put up on flat foundations laid directly onto the permafrost, and not on stilts, as is the normal practice in the arctic region, to provide ventilation under them; as the permafrost warms and gives way, houses begin to sink and walls crack.

The village council wants to move people to Inta and knock the barracks down, but the occupants resist - they have lived in much worse conditions. But, eventually people will have to move; the barracks will then be knocked down, and with them the twenty seven year history of Abez *lagiers* will sink into the permafrost. And once Victor is gone, who will speak for the cemeteries; who will want to come to an outpost on a railway line lost somewhere between the Russian tundra and taiga; and what will remain here to remind us of the "pit" - perhaps the bridge over the River Usa?

And the bridge is just ahead - seven segments span the river. It looks impressive from distance, solid and everlasting from close up. A small concrete marker nearby gives its date of birth – 1940; a broken wheel of a wheelbarrow lies nearby, but nowhere will you find any numbers for the broken lives of prisoners who built it. River Usa flows unperturbed by history, gleaming proudly in the northern sunshine; true, it did bring the prisoners here but eventually it did get rid of the jetties and the rail terminals biting into its side like vermin. The bridge is no impediment to its freedom; it will squeeze it with ice in winter, flood it in spring... who knows how long the bridge will last, but Usa will flow as ever.

The rail track runs straight as an arrow over the bridge and on top of the high embankment to the stop at Abez. On the riverbank and on low ground there is evidence of earlier construction activity - narrow-gauge rail tracks had run from the river to the village, an abandoned power line lies along the rail tracks, a skeleton of railway carriage rests in the middle of nowhere... Back in 1938-1941, construction was done with pick, shovel, and prisoners' muscles and its tempo was murderous; no cost and no lives were to be spared to meet the deadlines set by Stalin. The rail track followed the lay of the land, the path of least resistance - no embankments, no viaducts, no concern for safety... anything to meet the deadline - December 1941 for the first delivery of coal from Workuta. Later, repairs could and would be done, track layout straightened, bridges built, embankments raised, more men die...

But at the end of the day of tramping around Abez, I still find it impossible to imagine the scale of misery, pain and destruction of human life – a place where people died like flies. I have seen the cemetery; with Google I can see the trace of the perimeter of one of the *lagiers*, but all this is still not enough, for today, out in the open, the sun shines, meadows bloom with flowers, peace and silence surrounds.

And then, Victor shows me photographs - how it was then, in winter... And suddenly I knew, and you too would feel those atrocious conditions; you too would believe that prisoners did die like flies in this Abez, that this was their valley of tears, valley of death, that it was the pit... and that in the life of our fathers this Abez was their **Abyss.**

It's time for me to catch the train to Uhta; Victor and I walk the boardwalk to the train stop. A primitive building is set a little way on the other side of the tracks – one room, no windows, one bench hidden in total darkness waiting for a victim... no thank you, I will rather wait outside even if it rains, but it's a lovely sunset and the train is coming. Will it stop... will it... in this place of nowhere?

Back in the house, I left Victor a 1000 rouble note and now he gives me such a grateful hug... for a miserable £22! Surely, he deserves and needs 10 and 100 times more to support his work!

...and the train does stop - almost! I race as fast as the rucksack will allow me towards my designated wagon which happens to be at the far end, and I know I won't make it, for the whistle is already blowing impatiently... but a nearby carriage door suddenly opens and the guard yanks me in; just a fraction of a minute and the train is off. The guard, a big, blond, Russian woman just smiles. "Thank you! Thank you!" I stammer out of breath... I survived, I was the only one pulled out of this **Abyss**.

<u>Uhta (Ukhta), Yarenga, Sangaradok</u>

Oil! Heavy and viscous, almost like tar - but oil! Discovered in 1932 in the upper reaches of Yarega – a small river in the taiga – it gave life to Uhtpechlag with the remit to develop mineral resources in this region utilizing forced labour. By the time it was reorganized in January 1938, it had some 54,000 prisoners working in the Pechora basin. Its successor,

Uhta-Izhemsky ITL started life in Chibyu, a small village by the river Uhta. In January 1940, it had 20,000 prisoners and their numbers escalated rapidly to 39,000 by July 1941. Prisoners worked on oil, gas, asphalt, chemicals, brickworks and supporting infrastructure projects in *lagiers* scattered over a wide area in the Uhta-Sosnogorsk region. Chibyu expanded and in 1939 acquired the status of town - Uhta. It's a big town now, a thriving city really - 100,000 population.

Follow Leninski Prospect north-west and you come to an abrupt end of town. Just across the boundary road lies a vast open space covered with luscious grass and some shrubs. A small chapel and monument at its edge stands like a sentinel and stops the expansion of the city in this direction. Who would have guessed that this is the place where the Zabalotny (beyond the mud banks) *lagier* once stood; nothing remains of it but this open land - you could walk your dog there. Drive southeast through Chibyu, the old town, turn right at the roundabout and there's River Uhta – people picnicking, bathing, splashing, sunning themselves joyously on its shingly bank. No trace of GULAG history here, only some signs of heavy industry further up on the opposite bank.

Take a bus south-west to Yarega - the "oil city" - or rather a cluster of three oil mines in the taiga. The slag heap and the wheels above the shaft of mine #1 visible from afar will come as an incongruous surprise, for who and where in this world digs for oil. I have seen "nodding donkeys" bringing oil up from the ground; I have seen "Christmas trees" holding back oil and gas gushing from below ground, but actually mining oil like coal in deep underground mines? Perhaps here, the word GULAG or NKVD that made people cringe from fear has been substituted by a softer acronym borrowed from the English language: UHTA – "**Underground Heavy Tar Accumulations**"?

Father Albin Janocha[3], a Polish monk sentenced to twelve years labour, worked here in 1944-48. Shaft #1 and #3 were already operational at the time and shaft #2 was under construction. A large-diameter vertical shaft was being dug by the prisoners, and horizontal underground corridors then radiated from it ending in large chambers. Long bore holes were then drilled into the walls releasing very viscous oil into open channels flushed out with water for processing above ground. The redundant mining spoils were carted out to above ground and disposed of as land fill to provide a drier and firmer ground around the mines. Life at mine #3 was easier, especially in winter, for the *lagier* was right next to the mine and the *posiolek* – the settlement where the free workers lived - was adjacent.

Sixty-five years later, in 2011, all three mines are still operational. A young woman at mine #1 offers to take me to meet an old resident who may be able to tell me something about life as it had been here in the days of the GULAG. Elena remembers those days well; now retired, she lives in two rooms and kitchen that looks out onto the mine. With sunshine streaming in, and a visitor from England to listen to her story, a contented smile enlightens her face.

Back in those days they were recruiting for work in the mines; Elena came here in 1952 and worked in the mine all her life. *Women worked underground on equal terms with men: they were cutting corridors, boring holes in the walls and injecting hot water to flush out the oil... work was hard and dangerous so they* (the free people) *could retire at 50. After 1953, women worked above ground only. Mining spoils were removed in carts drawn by ponies; these poor animals were specially bred for this work, they lived and worked underground and never left the mine. It was good work; everyone was happy, good camaraderie, almost like a family, the bosses were very good, very considerate... You know, all bosses were "represyonovany" like most of the workers here - they were prisoners... There was a big fire in the mine here in 1953; many people died: our chief engineer, the gas technologist, and thirteen others died but it was all hushed up at the time... You know, if you want to see a lagier, there is one at shaft #3 in Domannik, but the old posiolek is in ruins. There are still some barracks here from those days: one is just behind the magazine and two more just across the road... Oh yes, there were Polish prisoners here too.*

Indeed, on the other side of the road nicely shaded by mature trees, stands a long barrack constructed from wooden planks, and a boardwalk runs along its length - all in a surprisingly good condition. A neatly dressed woman coming out of the barrack assures me - *it was built in 1941, certainly not later than early '40s; three families live in this barrack now, there's one more behind this and another behind the shop...*

But the thought of seeing a *lagier* close up excites my

imagination. It's a long walk to shaft #3 in Domannik - three miles of concreted road, and the sun is beating down.

The posiolek? Just follow the road and take the first turn left... And so I do - past the boiler house with a flourishing fountain in front of the administrative block and along the pavement shaded by trees on both sides; I turn left and... unbelievable, I can see what looks like a high wall enclosing a *lagier*! I can touch it! Solid wooden fence some eight feet high coils of barbed wire, watchtowers... I follow the wall cautiously... junk, disintegrating shacks strewn in the grass as if the *lagier* had been under siege. As I approach the corner, guard dogs pick up my scent and burst out of their sheds... big, vicious-looking brutes; chill runs up my spine but their leash held. I manage to get past them, round the corner, face the main entrance, and... no guards, no dogs, nothing! No one would expect a foreigner in his right mind to be loitering around a *lagier* – a prison - here with the intent of taking photographs, but I do.

A soldier comes out of the main entrance so I saunter up to him, as if I was on a Sunday leisure walk, to pre-empt any aggression from his side, but he's not interested – *go and see the nachalnik* (the boss) *if you want to see the lagier; the building is over there* - and walks away for a smoke.

A young officer happens to be standing by the building - sleek black hair, impeccable uniform. His face lights up and I can see amazement in his eyes as I tell him my story. He calls over the *nachalnik* – *listen, this man is from England, his uncle was imprisoned here in 1941... he would like to see the lagier... would you believe it!* The *nachalnik*, big and strong like a bull, looks at me coolly, not sure how to respond, but the young officer continues: *Can you come tomorrow? We will give you a lift to your hotel now. Come tomorrow at 10.30 promptly, it will be very interesting for us to hear your story, perhaps I can arrange for you to look inside the lagier from the first floor... but no photographs! Oh, you've been to Workuta? You know... there are three lagiers there - just out of town... You should see them... interesting.* He writes down his name, exact address of this place so a taxi will know where to bring me... How could I refuse? The board by the main entrance to the building reads:

Official Establishment of the Republic of Komi
Corrective Prison
#29

At 10.30 am next day, I am there and walk into the proverbial lion's den. Dark... silence... no one there to welcome me or kick me out... take a photo or two perhaps? But a plain-clothes man is coming down the stairs; he looks at my piece of paper with the name of the officer, disappears into a corridor and returns to tell me the officer is not available at the moment and his meeting is likely to last a long time! Surely, "my" officer would have known about it yesterday at the end of his working day. Evidently, old NKVD habits die hard.

How many times have I read about it – you may be there, outside *nachalnik's* office, standing, waiting, perhaps to plead help for your dying child, but *nachalnik* is busy, or not there – not for you! But I don't need to plead; I already have what I came for; I have taken photographs and video of the *lagier*... so I wait half an hour and leave. Certainly, I would have been nicely surprised if they had let me glimpse inside a *lagier* - Russia! Perhaps I should count myself lucky that I am still outside its walls?

The old Yarega *posiolek* is just a few yards away. It is in complete ruin. Here and there, grey, weathered and disintegrating timber dwellings lie prostrate while grass and shrubs penetrating their carcass add to an eerie ambience even in bright sunlight. Death of a *posiolek*, death of its people, but no cemeteries in the neighbourhood... A little further out, by what's left of the perimeter road, a more recent building in brick gapes at me as if begging for help, its windows smashed, doors wrenched out, floor strewn with glass, boarding and... books! I flick through the pages of several books - damp, the language is Russian, naturally; surely, I can save one book and take it home with me. A passer-by woman tells me gaily: *oh this was our village store, shop, library... it was built in 1983... why do you ask; you want to rent it?*

Back at the shaft, a little to the side, hidden amongst slim silver birch, I find an altogether different world. Several barracks, obviously old but perfectly maintained, their exterior timber walls in delicate milk-chocolate colours; all windows solidly in place. A ditch runs alongside, its banks covered in grass and a mass of lovely yellow flowers - a perfect setting except... I can smell oil. The water in the ditch is black, hardly flowing - surprising to see that mass of flowers blooming so happily in this oily water.

Walking back along the road to Yarega I can admire the forest from close up - tall, slim, silver birch in pale green leaves contrast sharply with the dark density of whatever lies behind them. But not for long, for automobiles coming towards me zigzag and sway in a frightening way as if they were challenging me to miss collision with them. But just one look at the road surface gives the reason - huge potholes and shoals of loose gravel are the real challenge!

Further along the road, again I can smell oil; black, thick oil burps in a pothole at the side of the road and flows sluggishly in the ditch. But all oil has value, and further ahead, men are laying a pipeline... *Hey, you! Shpion?* shouts a worker good-humorously at the sight of my camera. I wave back: niet, niet... tourist, tourist, not a spy!

The last-of-the-day workers' bus gives me a lift to Uhta. *Misha*, a young mechanic, is the only other passenger. He invites me to his home so I can phone the UK; his parents are preparing their evening meal and are surprised but happy to see a visitor from the UK. Try once, try twice... but the phone doesn't accept calls – they have just discovered that they are in arrears with payments! The young man takes me round to his relatives across the corridor; and here the phone does work, so I make the call and leave a 100-rouble note – the relief on their faces is obvious.

Of course *Misha's* parents insist on my having a meal with them. They place a large helping of scrambled eggs and potatoes on my plate but it's obvious that this is about all there is to eat tonight so, of course, I am not hungry and return most of what's on my plate to them – it's gone in an instant. As we drink tea, they sympathise with my search for the "Footprints of our Fathers". *Misha's* family originates from *Molodechno* in Ukraine; his grandfather was also *represyonovany* and died in some *lagier*, who knows where, but Russia is their home now and, they too, are thinking of writing down their family's history – so their children will know.

On the way to the bus stop, *Misha* and his father show me the new settlement ...*see these blocks; we moved in just in time. When Gorbachov came to power, all work stopped, and look what we have now: empty shells of buildings, no doors or windows... no one lives there, only rubbish and drugs and delinquents... OK, I won't spend much on beer* - says the father to Misha in a quiet voice as he parts with us.

Follow the river Uhta downstream, past the petroleum refinery, past the industrial zone, to *Dezhnevo*; talk to anyone, and they will tell you this area was full of *represyonovany* people – who else would have laid the railway tracks, built the rail bridge across the Uhta, worked in the building materials plant in such terrible conditions... All *lagiers* have been demolished by now and nothing of them remains today, but I do find one *lagier* still very much in use. A little beyond the village and right next to the road, its boundary wall, barbed wire and watchtowers are all clearly visible as if on public display – just an ordinary prison to-day, no more political prisoners in

Russia to-day? There was another *lagier* for *represyonovany* people in *Vetlosyan,* on the opposite side of the river and the cemetery was up on mount *Vetlosyan* - the airport is there now.

It would have been a long wait in the mid-day heat for a bus to take me back to Uhta but, thankfully, I am offered a lift by Yury, in his delivery van. *Sangaradok? Of course I know it - I was born there, my mother still lives there! It's no longer called Sangaradok - it's Shadgaradok now - the hospital is still there, but there's nothing left of the lagier.*

The only respite from murderous conditions in any *lagier* a prisoner could hope for was a few days in hospital, and *Sangaradok*, even today, is the "lungs" of Uhta. The old hospital buildings have been knocked down in 1976 and replaced by more modern facilities, but the disintegrating carcass of one or two of the original wooden houses still lying in the lovely wooded park give a hint of how it had been. The nearby *lagier* for women is also long gone but, amazingly, an entire street of houses dating from the 1940's still exists; they were built by the prisoners for the bosses and officers, and they are still occupied today - a remarkable piece of history.

Yury shows me around the house he had built himself - three rooms, refrigerator, carpets, garden full of flowers and vegetables, and introduces me to his mother... A photograph, may I? *No, no... I am not dressed properly... my hair...* But Yury has no such inhibitions and poses proudly for the record. On the way out, we stop at the municipal cemetery by the road, but the guard at its entrance tells me that graves from the 1940's would be impossible to find now.

On the way back from Sosnogorsk to Uhta I had a memorable glimpse of another live *lagier* through the window of my train. As it was passing the *lagier* wedged in between the rail tracks and the river Izhma, I could see right inside the perimeter walls - the death zones, the watchtowers, barbed wire and searchlights. At night, the searchlights mounted on the watchtowers were blindingly strong.

Back in Uhta, *Vladimir Nickolayewich*, professor of history at Uhta University, is happy to talk about local history. There is really nothing left to see of the GULAG *lagiers* now; possibly something at *Syrochayskaya colonia*, Camp #13 is now *Kirpichny posiolek*... but they are all quite far from Uhta and roads are so bad that even taxi drivers will be reluctant to go there. But he does have some old photographs on an undeveloped film that may be of interest, so he will take a look.

Eugenia Anatolivna looks after the Memorial Museum of the GULAG at the University – perhaps the most important item here is the thick volume of names and details of people executed in Stalin's time, photographs and life-summaries of scientists are also displayed but there is very little to depict the life and conditions in a GULAG *lagier*.

At the end of the day I leave Uhta with the impression the town now lives completely detached from its history of the first half of the 20th century, as if everything was normal, as if there was no pain, no fear, no brutality and cruelty, no work beyond endurance, no hunger, no death... The slate has been wiped clean - a monument here, another there... nothing left to understand or to make you cringe. Yet Uhta was the centre of the Uht-Izhemskyi ITL, one of the largest Gulags in the Komi Republic.

Some facts extracted from official sources show just how fickle life under Stalin had been:

Back in 1936, a group of Russian oil industry professionals was sent for six months to the United States to study the search, exploration and exploitation of oil and gas fields. A detailed report was published in the book "American Oil Industry." But by the end of the 1930's, two consecutive 5-year plans failed to meet the commitments of planned oil production in the whole of USSR, so the entire group that travelled to study in the USA were shot, only one man was spared.

The 17th International Geological Congress was held in Moscow in July 1937. From amongst Russian Geologists participating in the Congress, 11 were shot, 42 arrested, 4 repressed, 2 exiled, 1 committed suicide, 1 escaped. The typical death rate in all GULAG *lagiers* over the years was in the range 2-4% but some periods were truly shocking. In 1942 and 1943, 24.9% and 22.4% of prisoners perished, respectively.

Indeed, the scene of people sunning themselves on the bank of river Uhta, or Elena in Yarega with a contented smile on her face, or Fr. Albin writing about his four years in the oil mines of Yarega as if it was a normal assignment in the service of God... all are so incongruous with Uhta of the 1940-1950's. To the people I met here, the word "GULAG" with all its connotations belongs to distant history now; it is no longer a part of their lives. Perhaps only in the case of *Misha* and his father, the GULAG is still palpable; its meaning sits just under their skin.

4

Footprints in Kazakhstan

After mass in Jarevo, in the chapel of a small village in Belarus only a few kilometres from my birthplace, the starting point of my trail, the sacristan came up to me - *you know... my father perished in Kazakhstan... All I know is that he was in Kingir, Jezkazgan district. I hear you are going there... could you perhaps try to find out something?*

How could I refuse? His and my father could well have left their homes on the same day, followed the same route to Lithuania and travelled in the same wagon of the same train to the same *lagier* perhaps. But somewhere along the trail their paths diverged... and thank God they did, for the *lagier* in Kingir had a particularly nasty and bloody history; my father made it to Buzuluk, his didn't.

It's a long, long way from Jarevo to Kingir, and the wheels of my train go on and on and on, drumming that dire refrain: death-*lag*... death-*lag*... death-*lag*... Day one, two... five... Minsk, Moscow, Samara, Orenburg, Chelyabinsk, Petropavlovsk, Kokshetau, Astana, Karaganda, and it's still a long 500km. to Jezkazgan...

Early morning... my train from Karaganda is approaching its destination. The sun is already well up; barren, brown-red land stretches to the horizon on my left and right. As the train approaches Jezkazgan I can see signs of large-scale mining activity:

long embankments of mining spoils, heavy plant and machinery enclosures, pylons, a huge power generating station and other indefinable industrial installations shrouded in heavy pollution. And suddenly, from beyond the wide strip of heavy industry and the opaqueness of pollution, emerges a huge cross on raised ground... I am amazed. A cross! You wouldn't see it in Stalin's days, or in Khrushchev or Brezhnev days. Had you asked for a cross to be put up to commemorate those perished in GULAG *lagiers*, why, they would happily have you crucified on it, and have your bones add lime to its foundations!

Fr. Victor meets me at the station and takes me to his home for breakfast. A low, grey house with tin-covered roof stands indistinguishable from other houses in this neighbourhood of unpaved streets full of ruts and potholes. A part of this house is sectioned off and serves as a prayer house - yet no one would have guessed that, for the local authorities have not given permission to put up a cross or any other public sign on the building.

Without any hesitation, Fr. Victor takes me on a tour of the places I need to see. The original Kingir *posiolek* has been absorbed into what is today the town of Jezkazgan. The *lagier* of the 1940's and 50's was demolished and covered over to obliterate all traces of its existence and of the revolt of the prisoners in 1953/4 so infamously put down by Khrushchev's tanks and machineguns. The effacement of the *lagier* was so effective that, by the early 1990's, no one knew exactly where it stood and where the burial ground was. Much later, someone wanted to build a large depot or factory, and when ground clearing started, masses of bones were uncovered; they were gathered, removed and now lie in the mound on which stands the cross I saw from the train as it was approaching Jezkazgan.

The history of Kingir needs to be told separately, for it is saturated with the blood and lives of its prisoners. Nothing remains of it today. Only the memorials erected on the mound of human bones testify to Stalin's legacy. The landmark cross I saw from the train commemorates Lithuanians perished in the strikes of May 1954; other monuments commemorate the Ukrainians, Russians, and of so many other nations.

Yet a Kingir *posiolek* does exist! It lies just outside the town of Jezkazgan, but it turns out to be a new, almost a model *posiolek*, built in late 1960's - there is a cemetery there too. One wonders why this *posiolek* bears the name "Kingir" so prominently displayed at the entrance - surely, it couldn't have been so named to commemorate its bloody history! On the contrary, was it not to derail tourists and researches; was it not there to conceal the truth and the history of Kingir?

Kingir - Rudnik

Not far from Kingir *posiolek* lies its associated mining *lagier* - Rudnik; its ruins are clearly visible from the road. All barbed wire enclosures, all watch towers have gone; all roofs, doors, windows have long been stripped out; only rubble remains now - no one wants it, no one needs it in this part of Kazakhstan. The imposing façade of the administration building still stands, and its date of birth stamped with the Soviet star is proudly registered on the front - 1940.

The isolator has been demolished but its pit some ten feet deep is still there - unmistakable. And inside this huge *lagier* and the many ruined barracks only one vestige of prisoners' life was left behind - a metal slush bucket! But just outside the *lagier* boundary, discarded shoes, cloth, bits of metal, plastic and other items that in normal life would have been seen as rubbish or junk, line the ditch separating the *lagier* from the world. And you may well wonder whether all this junk was discarded by the prisoners or removed by their guards, for they all knew that it would no longer be needed once the prisoners crossed the road.

And it's across the road from the *lagier* that the enormity of what went on here really strikes home. As I walk the copper-hued ground, sparsely covered with tufts of wizened grass and masses of stone chippings, I dare not kick a stone, or dig my foot into the ground for fear of striking a skull or uncovering human bones… I am treading on a vast burial ground. Mounds of earth are clearly visible on this flat terrain, some large and more pronounced than others; graves for one, or ten, or perhaps a hundred dead left untouched for fifty years now lie weathered but still discernible - no flowers had ever lain there. A shred of discoloured cloth emerges from the earth - is it marking a grave? A strand of rusty barbed wire lies partly buried – why… who was girdled with it?

One might have overlooked the mounds and treated

these acres as wasteland, a hunting ground for vermin perhaps, but further down the incline a few crosses and metal enclosures have survived; rectangular clumps of shrubbery grow here and there marking the graves of the winter-dead, when the ground was frozen rock-hard, when only very shallow graves were dug. Somewhere amongst these shallow graves lies the father of the sacristan in Jarevo... but where exactly amongst the several thousand buried here — who will ever know?

But the living have not forgotten this burial ground. A large simple cross has been erected to mark this place and, for the past few years in July, crowds visit here to pray, to remember, to reflect on the evil which shrouds this past. The cross is white covered with black marks over its entire surface - what do they represent? Are they to connect the dead with their homeland... represented by the *beriozka*, the national tree of Russia? Or do they perhaps represent the number of graves here - and of these, there were too many to count.

Deathly silence envelops this vast open space only rarely disturbed by the sound of a passing motor car... A huge photograph of life and death from early nineteen-fifties unfolds at your feet... like then, characteristic hues of charcoal-grey and browns predominate, except here they take on a more sinister, darker, bloody shades, almost maroon in places in their intensity; clumps of scrub in dead-green add depth and shadows; the air is still; the sky deep-blue punctured by solitary tall, elegant, round mining shaft towers with rectangular openings... You know what's under your foot and still, you are not angry, no hatred in your heart... your soul and mind at peace... look around; look for an answer... why?

Not many from this Rudnik would have reached Buzuluk in time to enlist in the Anders Army... and there were so many other places such as Kingir in and around Karaganda – in Fedorovka, in Spaask... where prisoners worked their arms off, and lost their health and lives in open-pit coal mines, copper mines and smelters, power generating stations and railroad construction... no, not many from these places reached Buzuluk.

Fedorovka - Karaganda

Fedorovka was born of coal – black; its future history stamped with Stalin's callous thumbprint. I didn't need to ask; I could see in the distance that huge embankment carrying railway tracks. I couldn't see the cemetery camouflaged by shrubs but, sure enough, the mass of graves was there, along the embankment, hugging its side, almost tucked underneath it.

Walk amongst the graves... one item, one cross amongst the hundreds, gives the Fedorovka story away. A sturdy wooden cross with a heavily rusted metal plate attached to it, still stands upright in the ground; no name on the plate, no date, only a number – 5248! And where are the other 5247 graves? Where are their bones, their names, dates of birth and departure? Buried in the pits under the embankment perhaps - human skeletons cementing the rubble... useful even after death? Or perhaps drowned in the huge open coal pits, now filled with water? Fedorovka - a GULAG *lagier*. Stalin - a wart on Mankind!

But in the late afternoon of a day in June, wherever you look, the ground is covered in lush green, cattle graze contentedly, people work on their plots of land, the rail track curves graciously into the horizon; only the hoot of a train engine from an already-forgotten history disturbs the peace... and you wonder: Fedorovka - a GULAG *lagier*? Really?

True, today Fedorovka is no longer a *lagier*. The barbed wire is gone, the watch towers are gone, armed guards are gone too, and so are their dogs; hunger and misery have abated... But people are still alive who remember the Fedorovka of 1938, and the 40's, people who were part of the hunger, sickness and freezing cold, part of the condemned labour.

The prisoners were corralled behind barbed wire enclosures in huge camps - men in one camp, women and children in another, adjoining. They were Germans, Poles, Ukrainians, even Japanese, intelligentsia and factory workers, kulaks and peasants, criminals and murderers - their arms and legs were the one common factor. They were here to work, to dig coal for the industries in the Urals, for the glory of Stalin's Russia. And they were worked to death in huge open-cast coal mines; they dug, and kept on digging wider and deeper, and deeper still, until water broke through the bottom and flooded the mine. Machinery was abandoned, people were abandoned... how many of the 5247 rest here? Who knows, who cared, who dared to write about it?

Those that survived were somehow able to bribe, to smuggle things or inmates in or out, to sell something they cherished, somehow able to make friends - they were the born survivors. And at long last their fortune turned, if not for the prisoners of the 1940's and 50's then for their children and grandchildren. After the breakup of the USSR, from the early 1990's onwards, Fedorovka Germans and the Poles began returning to their Homeland, but for so many others Fedorovka is their home, Kazakhstan their Homeland. But there is no requirement now for neither forced nor free labour, there is no coal here now, the open cast mines lie flooded, black, placid, a painful reminder of Fedorovka's history.

Walking amongst the barracks of Fedorovka today it's hard to imagine life as it was in the 1940's. The administrative building, the social building and the refectory, and the barracks are still there, all solidly built in brick by Japanese prisoners - single storey but of pleasing architecture, once painted distemper white, now tarnished by time and their history, all nicely settled amongst shrubbery. But the utter misery of the 1940's has been replaced by the utter misery of today. Drugs, alcoholism, broken families, unmarried mothers, orphans... rubbish piled high in the yards and along the passageways between the barracks, cracks in walls, communal standpipe for drinking water... children play football with rubbish heaps for goal posts, dogs scavenge... A still pretty, blond, young woman happily poses for a photo and would happily give much more for just a few dollars more...

a matron stands at the entrance to the "street" keeping an eye on it all. An old cobbler from Georgia sweats at his living in a workshop no bigger than 5x8 feet. A group of youths walks through a mass of rubbish piled high towards the black lagoons… no, not to school, to fish for lunch and supper, to stay alive.

Spaask - Karaganda

Spaask – what, where, when, why… a GULAG *lagier* here? It's so easy to miss the two or three wooden crosses barely keeping their arms and head above the lush grass covering this area. Who could have guessed that this is a vast burial ground? Who knows how many perished in this *lagier*, who kept statistics then, who cared when bodies, in their tens, were carted daily from the *lagier* to be dumped here - no cross, no name, not even a number plate. But Spaak's history has not been forgotten, and with the coming of *Glasnost*, the French, Polish, Azerbaijanis, and so many other nations, erected monuments in remembrance of the tragedy here.

And not far, just a kilometre or so away, the white of *lagier* barracks cuts sharply against the green of the gently rolling hills – these are military barracks now, and woe to anyone caught snooping around with a camera. Just a little further away, the blackened remains of an earlier *lagier*, perhaps dating from the 1930's, are still visible, and a little further still, but hidden from view, lies the Spaasky Zavod - the copper smelter, built and operated by the British back in the late 1920's and 1930's, then taken over by the Soviets, now in Kazakhstan, and still working today.

In 1932, Spaask was absorbed into the Karaganda group of *lagiers* - the *Karlag*. In 1941 it became a *speclag* - the *lagier* for "special" prisoners, under special, restrictive rules. Stalin's thumbprint was now firmly stamped on it. The prison population of Karaganda exploded and the burial ground began to fill with prisoners of war, political dissidents, criminals, and invalids.

In the first three years of its existence, the *lagier* expanded from some 1500 prisoners to well over 10,000 prisoners of some forty nationalities. Everyone had to work in the quarries supplying building materials for the expanding *lagier*; even those without arms were harnessed like cattle to pull four-wheeled wagons laden with rocks from quarries. Epidemics struck the exhausted prisoners: dysentery in 1949-50 and then contagious yellow fever in 1951. Human cattle carted dead humans to the burial ground. No material for crosses, no time for digging graves, time only for one massive common grave in the steppe.

At last, after Stalin's death, conditions in Spaask began to ease: more food, more humane treatment of prisoners, and rising hope for release at the end of one's sentence. Eventually, by 1956, essentially all political prisoners were released. In the ten years of its existence, some 40,000 prisoners of many nationalities, including many Polish prisoners amongst them, tasted the tragedy of life in Spaask.

One man I met along my trail did return from Karaganda to his native Postawy in 1956, to my birthplace... but no one wanted him there, there was no work for him there, no bread for him there. He was a "convicted criminal" like my father, sentenced to labour in a GULAG *lagier*; he was "*represyonovany*", and that label - "*represyonovany*" - written into his identity card was like that other label - "*tut washa moghila*" - firmly stuck onto the backs of men on Kola Peninsula; it stuck to him too - for life. In the end, he had no choice but to return to Karaganda! There, he was one of many; amongst his own people; there he could work... in any *lagier;* there he could live - just.

But copper and coal were essential to fuel Stalin's ambition and for the war effort in 1941-5, so very few from Spaask or Fedorovka, or Kingir in Jezkazgan were "amnestied" and released in time to make their way to the Anders Army, but others, from the remotest parts of Stalin's empire, kept coming.

5

Tut Washa Moghila – This is Your Grave

Rat tat tat... rat tat tat... rat tat tat... No, no... it's not machinegun fire - not yet, not today... It's the wheels of the train from Wilno, or Kozielsk, or from so many other stations in Russia going on, and on, and on... to GULAG *lagiers* on the Kola Peninsula.

And the train rolled north - 60 men crammed into each cattle wagon, starving and dying of thirst and suffocation. Seven days later the train stops; men stagger out into the open - Murmansk - end of May 1941. Those who still had the strength, had to struggle a further nine kilometres from the station to a holding place inside barbed wire fencing under open skies. Those who survived to tell the story, remember this place as the "Valley of Tears" or the "Valley of Death". And this was just the beginning.

Two weeks later, the next *etap* was ready for them; they marched the 9km. to the port of Murmansk, were crammed into the ship "Staliniec" and despatched on another "leisure" trip - this time, around the nose of the Kola Peninsula to a "welcoming" party at the mouth of River Ponoi. Can you imagine being eaten alive by huge rats; there was no respite as they gnawed and scavenged at their feet, for they too were starving?

But who wants to remember that now? Who talks about it now? Just take a look at the internet; look up

Kola Peninsula, look up Ponoi... what do you see, what do you read? What do tour operators propose? Salmon fishing in the River Ponoi - the best in the world! See the rich Americans, their faces beaming with delight? They will also entice you with fantastic skiing on the slopes of the beautiful Khibiny Mountains, or an adventure across the rivers, swamps, lakes and the beautiful taiga that smells and feels, and still is, almost virgin, unexplored territory even today; you will be jostled in 4x4's and massive ex-army trucks, for only such can meet the challenge.

They will show you a village of Pomorcy, or rather, what is left of the coastal settlers who have lived here for centuries. They will show you the desert - yes, an expanse of yellow sand in the tundra north of the Arctic Circle where the wind uncovers the dead in the graves of the village cemetery and heaps sand dunes onto the living! Or they will offer to take you to visit a genuine village of the Saami People, the Lapps – to sleep in their abodes, taste their food, see their culture on display in museums; and if you come in winter, you will see them herding reindeer. And, oh, there is so much more...

Who, today, wants to hear about the GULAG camps on Kola; about the spill-over *lagiers* from the Solovetsky Islands as early as the 1920's; or about the 800km. long telephone line strung across the Kola Peninsula from Murmansk to the mouth of the Ponoi where you could not have got lost for, if you could not see the telegraph poles, you could follow the skeletons of those who laid the line.

Who wants to hear about the forcible collectivization of the Lapps, about their resistance, about the fate they suffered at the hands of Lenin and Stalin; or about the brutal relocation inland of the Pomorcy people from the Barents Sea coast in the north of Kola to make room for the now-defunct military installations on that coast? No… you will be talking to the second or third post-Stalin generation on Kola; they too want to work, to live in the modern world, not necessarily to be drunk, unemployed, without hope… They simply want to be just like you and me, or better still, like the rich Americans… if only they could!

Why would you want to look at the detritus from mining for nickel, or for Apatite in Kirovsk and Apatity? Would you not rather stand on the summit of the beautiful Khibiny Mountains, breathe the fresh air, look at the panorama at your feet, or savour the thought that you are well inside the Arctic Circle, or reflect on the uniqueness of this place?

And if you happen to be in Murmansk today, you may well marvel at this large, modern city north of the Arctic Circle – at its museums and the port of Murmansk that stays open and free of ice throughout the winter. But ask for the "Valley of Tears" or the "Valley of Death" - people will know of it; you will get directions, but not to the "Valley of Tears" where my father and so many other fathers wept from loss of hope…

By a very clever subterfuge, Stalin's regime designated another place the "Valley of Death", a place west of

Murmansk, close to the border with Finland, where the battle front between the German and Soviet armies came to a stalemate. You cannot miss it; you cannot miss the expositions of Russian battle hardware, tanks, guns, cemeteries and huge monuments to the glory of the great and brave Russian soldiers. But who, seventy years later, will know of that other "Valley of Death" just a few kilometres from the railway station in Murmansk?

GULAG-72 km.

I was fortunate, history understood and smiled at me this day; Ivan knew the place of a long-forgotten derelict GULAG *lagier*; his colleague, Petia offered to take me there... if I dare - just the two of us.

So... how did I get there? What are the roads like - you may ask. Well... if you were made of rubber – you would have gone right through the metal roof; if you carried a lot of fat on your body – you would have lost most of it along the way; if you were of skin and bones – you would have found blue marks all over them; if you could have peeled a strip of your skin – you would have seen the hundreds of perforations from mosquito bites... and they were hungry, for there were no other blood donors except the two human asses; even the bears took shelter in deeper woods. And yet, the trip was fascinating, exciting, memorable... an adventure I would never forego and would be happy to repeat, even the moments when the truck fell into a pothole full of murky water, tilted 25° and stuck! Water flooded 1/3 of the truck and my rucksack... I had to wade out through this murky, muddy water onto "dry" land.

But it's at moments like this that, suddenly, a thought flashes through my mind: I am following in the footsteps of our fathers… and enjoying it, finding it exhilarating, a broad smile on my face!

Am I not perverse - the worst kind of traveller? I don't kiss the ground our fathers trod; I don't kneel or pray, or lift my fists in anger clamouring for revenge. For here, our fathers were on an *etap*, trudging in a column from one GULAG camp to another, guarded and hustled by armed guards and vicious dogs… hungry, exhausted, dressed in rags, carrying their possessions. There was no smile on their faces; their eyes stared blankly into the distance; their legs and feet covered in sores buckled under the strain, no anti-mosquito sprays… and that warning constantly ringing in their ears: one step to the right or left out of the column, and we shoot - to kill! And I am following in their footsteps… happy in my soul to be retracing their *etap* despite the mosquitoes, the engulfing puddles, and the austerity of the surroundings.

If you prefer the rough, the wild, the wilderness camouflaged by woods, the heat and mosquitoes and mites, deep ruts and potholes camouflaged by huge puddles, torrents across your track… if you prefer all that to the comfort of even the lowest-grade hotel and the predictability of a pre-arranged trip then, undoubtedly, this trip, this awful *etap* is for you. Or if you like streams of crystal clean water, views of open lakes with magical reflections… you will find them here too; be an adventurer; walk the *etap*, if you dare!

But if you were here alone surrounded by the utter silence, your soul free to just gaze at what's around you... you would then begin to feel what our fathers must have felt. Your mind would focus on the endless kilometres of the railway line they were forced to build, the embankments they raised, the telephone and electricity lines they laid through swamps and streams and forest. You would see railway bridges swept away by torrents; you would see the carcass of an old steam engine swept off the rails... and you would know for sure that, in these conditions, many of our fathers must have perished. And you would look, and look... but find not even one cemetery, or burial mound... and the smile would fade on your face.

And, perhaps with great relief, you would see clear signs of the final victory of Capitalism over Communism in the 1990's: steel rails removed, telegraph poles abandoned to nature now look like tumbled crucifixes strung with wires, the entire railway abandoned, unwanted; no longer competitive in the world ruled by market economy; nobody walks the *etap* now. Our fathers' labour, their blood, sweat and tears, and lives - gone to waste, forgotten... left for travellers like me to rediscover and ponder.

If you were to follow the rail tracks, and if you knew where to look, you would come to the place where they had come to, where their lives had come to an end in the 1940's and 50's... you would have found the remains of a GULAG *lagier*; and you would find here the shreds of history of peoples' lives, pain, sickness and death. Your heart will race in great excitement, adrenalin will flow; you will dart here, there, everywhere; your camera will click away... for you have, at last, found visible, touchable shreds of our fathers' history - their footprints - you would have found what's left of GULAG-72km.

Now you can take a break, light a fire, bite into that thick slab of black bread, *slonina,* and smoked salmon; watch in amazement the midnight sun set the forest ablaze, and then bed down for the sun-lit night in a forester's wagon. But overnight, the gravity of what you saw on this day will overcome all your excitement, and you will know you have to go back to see, to feel... to share a moment with the ghosts of our fathers.

Now you see the perimeter fence still in place, barbed wire still cuts as it did then, and that *wyshka* - the hallmark of any *lagier* - still stands upright, but the guards have gone, the machineguns gone, the searchlight gone, cables dangle loosely, its step ladder leans at a mad angle... no, you wouldn't want to try climbing up there. And here, there, and there, and there... you see collapsed barracks; grey, rotten timber cracks under your foot; you see death and decay on large scale; that deathly silence and the greyness surrounding you is unnerving.

Wow - you nearly fell into it! A pit, dug deep, yawns at you from under a roof of poles covered with earth at ground level... its gaping, collapsed entrance beckons you in and would welcome you today as it welcomed so many in the 1940's! Surely, this pit was no living quarters, more a grim prison inside a prison - an isolator - cold, wet, black, suffocating.

And there! Just here! Two semicircular, large, black gaping holes glare at you from a mound of earth... and the cadaver of a grey, wooden "something" lies prostrate in front of them as if swallowed, digested and regurgitated by the hidden monster. Of course... the ovens! They had to bake their own bread!

And as you pace the length of the 200m perimeter fence, the next *wyshka* becomes discernible amongst the trees, its cabin blown off and the entire structure is listing badly. And just here, the posts and barbed wire of the inner fence are recognizable too. Yes, it's the death zone - the five-metre space between the outer and inner fence. If you were suicidal, just step into this space, and the guard in the *wyshka* would have immediately obliged you with a bullet. And those piles of stones and boulders lying here, there and there... what are they? Are they the corner stones or foundations for the barracks, or... or do they mark the pits, the final resting place of the many that perished here? No one lives to tell.

But eventually, you will have to stop, get that weight off your chest, start breathing, get your bearings. Call out loud... and you will be answered only by - silence. And suddenly, you will be struck by the realization that no cry of pain or cry for help, no prayer could ever have been heard outside the boundaries of this *lagier*, nor will it ever penetrate this dense, immovable volume of air suffocating the camp; here the air doesn't vibrate - trees cushion all.

As you look around, alone, the silence becomes over-powering, the greyness becomes over-powering... Momentarily you will become immobilized by its history... my father... was he here? If he was, thank God he got out - so many didn't.

The *lagier* has been taken over by self-seeded birch: slim, tall, silver, white, covered in new leaves... one tree for each departed soul? Even the sunrays that penetrate the thicket cannot dispel that oppressive and claustrophobic feeling until... you look at the ground! You are stepping on the most beautiful natural carpet. Forget the best of Persian carpets! None can compete with Nature, and none have soaked up as much blood, sweat and tears as the carpet under your feet, an amazing agglomeration of white, cream, brown, red, green moss and lichen woven into a fantastic mosaic of miniature flowers... deep and soft, tender almost. You will want to touch it, caress it... and in return, it would welcome you as it must have welcomed our fathers, yet nowhere in the area is there any evidence, not even a mound, of a cemetery or burial. And how many of our fathers never left this place? This will haunt your thoughts, yet you will want to return here just to sit in solitude, in this deathly silence and try to understand why... this inhumanity of Man to Man?

But there are places along the trail to GULAG-72km. where you would find yourself simply having to stop, to absorb an entirely different experience. A *wyshka*! Just a hundred metres off the road, on higher ground and towering well above even the tallest trees... no prison guards up on top, no machine guns trained on you, no vicious dogs minding its feet; on the contrary, it invites you to come and marvel at the infinite taiga. I have climbed a 67m. telecoms *wyshka* - but that was two years ago, and it was of welded steel construction... but this! Only half the height but most certainly not half as easy to climb - a remarkable Meccano job from tree trunks and nails! A feat of carpentry, construction and erection skills – no mechanical cranes at the time - only muscle power and ingenuity.

Step on rung one, two... 27... and, suddenly, all hell breaks loose around me! Miniature dive-bombers like the *Stukas* of the *Luftwaffe* fall out of the sky, charge me and at the last moment veer away; the forest, forever in silence and composure, suddenly erupts screaming. It's a live scene taken from Hitchcock's film "The Birds", and they are attacking me – me, not some actor in a film! Crows...? How could crows survive winter temperatures of -40°C; surely they are not migratory birds?

I "freeze" my hands onto the 4" beams of the tower, and by sheer willpower, I can just about stop fear numbing my brain. I crane my neck, and there, directly above my head – a crows' nest! If I were a boy of some ten or twelve, I would have poked a stick into the nest and watched the crow's entire domain break up into shreds on the way down to the foot of the *wyshka*. I can imagine that bemused look on my face and my surprise that life can be so easily destroyed; but now, at seventy-two... I am ready to let live and hope to live - a little longer?

With both feet back on the ground, I feel relieved, safe, happy, smiling... and Nature smiles back at me. I did not sin! It has shown me the taiga in its fearful magnificence; soft, warm, appreciative rays of sun enliven the delicate green of silver birch in spring, and there, in the far, far distance lie the magnificent *Lovozerskoye Tundry* like a huge grey whale streaked with layers of snow... But still, Man remains Nature's implacable enemy for, first with axes, now with chain saws Man cuts away at its life leaving huge patches of eczema on its surface, and in retaliation, the taiga is merciless to anyone lost in its embrace.

And to make that point in the confrontation between Nature and Man, at the very top of the *wyshka* sits not the hammer & sickle of its constructors, nor a cross or cockerel, or the double-headed black eagle of the Tsar of Russia but a black crow! It had driven this invader away, it had won!

But what was the fate of the master-builders of this formidable *wyshka* - did they survive? Did they find their way home through this immense taiga, did they win their reprieve, or did they perish?

And if it were not for the crows, if I had been allowed to climb to the very, very top of the tower and look hard into the distance to penetrate the secrets of this foreboding yet magnificent taiga... how many similar *lagiers* would I have seen, how many patches of eczema, how many, stone quarries... rail tracks? Many are hidden forever but some still thrive. The word "GULAG" might have already merged into history, but men still labour – not for Stalin now, but for Capitalism, in Kirovsk, in Revda… in so many *lagiers* throughout Russia.

<u>Kirovsk.</u>

Polish people have a saying: "*z motyką na księżyc*" - a task as futile as prospecting for minerals "with pick & shovel on the moon". And yet, the Soviets did it – not on the moon, but they did here, in – Kirovsk.

How many hundreds of prisoners have been forced to chip away at the mountain with picks and shovels to get at the phosphate minerals here – Apatite – in the 1930's and 40's? My father could well have been one of them… But today, Man is impatient; the picks & shovels and the lives of those wielding them have been replaced by dynamite and heavy machinery; and half the mountain is gone! Look at it from a birds-eye view… and you might be looking at the landscape of the moon: barren, pockmarked, grey. The Americans have cut up a mountain in Nevada, but there, the mountain stands proud of its people and proud of its Presidents; here - the mountain weeps. It's a heart-wrenching sight: an avalanche of chippings, as if tears, rolls down its face, grey from pain… did Man do this to you?

The mine - *Kirovsky Rudnik* - stands at the foot of the mountain – contented, proud to have been cutting up the mountain since 1929. It will take all the tears that the mountain can shed, process them, and sell them to you and me. Somewhere around Kirovsk were the *lagiers,* prisoners and the NKVD - no sign of them now. Who can tell how many lives were shed, like the 'tears' of this mountain, into the grave pits at its base?

A touch of orange, beige, milk-chocolate colours… a fresh coat of paint on workers' residential and administrative blocks; its history has been repainted, given a new look, new interpretation - isn't it all so pretty! But on the way back to Kirovsk town, just look north, across the lake… see those miserable, abandoned barracks? The old thermal power station still works and belches out smoke, blacker than the greyness of Khibiny Mountains; the buildings and life around it are long dead.

A well known Russian film producer - Nickolay Dostal – set out to pass on to posterity Lenin's and Stalin's legacy in his film "Lenin's Testament". The film was shot at the abandoned Lovchorr mine near Titan, Kirovsk - at the actual place where the *lagier* once stood. Some of the original barracks still stood there in 2004, others were reconstructed, barbed wire and towers were added to reflect camp conditions as they were in the 1940's. The "Memorial" Foundation wanted to acquire the camp from the film producer, but local authorities didn't want a permanent exhibition of all that was wrong with Lenin's legacy; today, only a flat area, strewn with rock chippings, remains where the camp once stood - the top of the mountain has been chipped away flat!

But near Perm, a long way north-east of Moscow, one of the GULAG *lagiers* has been returned to its Stalin-era state. It is now a "Museum of the

GULAG", better known as Perm-36. The perimeter fence, barbed wire, guard towers and death zones, barracks with tiered wooden banks, administrative buildings... are all there now for all to see - all clean, all sanitized. Only the NKVD, the guards, their dogs, and the prisoners have been removed - no longer there to shock the world.

But what good is a replicate GULAG *lagier*? Who will see life as it really was in a *lagier*, in a real barrack? Can you smell the stench of sweat, urine and filth saturating prisoners' rags; will you see rats scurrying across the floor and your body? Will you ever know how you would react if, in the night, you were drenched by a cascade from the bunk above where a man has just expired? Or when, in the middle of the night, you suddenly felt a cold blade against your throat and a thief taking all that's precious to you – would you freeze from fright, or struggle? Can you guess how long you would take to begin to sleep comfortably with lice sucking you dry in bed, or bugs falling onto your face from above, or men sitting naked on wooden bunks sanitizing their rags by crushing lice between their fingernails? What would you do when you realized that the thugs on the bunk opposite are playing cards - for your rags, or your eyes, or your life? Would you not lick the soup bowls left by others, or suck the bones of fish thrown away by others, or rummage in the filth outside the kitchen or canteen when you've been assigned to *kociol #1* - the lowest level of nourishment - because you can no longer do the norm? And when your health is gone, your strength is gone and you are amongst the living-dead, would you still struggle, still want to live, still clutch onto life... even though you have been told many times over that you have been brought here to work, and to die here? And would you still let yourself be kicked out of your bunk at 04.00 and drag yourself to work for your executioner, in the mines, on the railway line, or felling trees...? How can we feel any of this by looking around a Museum?

Revda

I am trying to make some sense of the schedule for coaches from Revda to Murmansk displayed on the wall of a building; a big black Audi just stands there, parked... its driver sits idle, watching... perhaps he can help?

Yes, of course! Ivan can do much more than just explain the coach schedule; in fact, he could take me all the way to Murmansk – but that would cost a lot! But if I want to see the Revda mine... sure, he can take me there - no customers for the Audi today, so why not?

We float the few kilometres to the mine majestically, as befits a big black Audi in this part of the world, and park right in front of the guardhouse. They know Ivan... yes O.K. he can take me up the mountain... *but, Ivan, are you sure he is not a spy from the West?* - shouts the guard at the last moment.

And so, we take the path towards the top of the hill; but I have to stop every few metres – not because I am tired - because the tundra here in spring is simply arresting. On the way up, Ivan explains why all boulders and large stones on this side of the hill face in a particular direction, tells me the name of this and every other clump of flowers, which berries are edible and when they will ripen… but I know that none of these details will stay in my head for long, for with my eyes open wide, every step up the track brings excitement and a broader smile to my face.

There's some kind of magic woven into the carpet covering this barren tundra - some magic in the play of colours, of the fresh and delicate green of the grass, of the quiet yellows, the reds, the white… the flowers, all in miniature, all embedded in a background of - grey. It's the grey-that is so arresting - the "living-grey" of the rocks at my feet, of the distant tundra, of the sky even… of the grey in the lives of the prisoners chipping at the rock… but still holding onto life. A setting both beautiful and painful at the same time, like the blend of the black and white, of happiness and the depths of misery in the life of our fathers…

An arresting panoramic view - both wondrous and shocking - rivets you in place every few steps up the hill. Look straight ahead and you only see the tundra in its spring magnificence, but to my left - half the mountain is gone! Man, with his bulldozers and trucks is still winning here. Grey tears of rock chippings roll down the mountain to the processing plant at its feet - itself grey, covered in dust, corroded, brutal. And to my right, partly hidden by the shoulder of the mountain, lies a large lake, placid, dense, lifeless, grey - the washings, the rejects, the effluent from the mine.

Well down below, on the far side of the road where I

saw only that wondrous tundra, Ivan points out the remnants of a GULAG *lagier* – all traces of life and its history have been removed; nothing but rubble remains now... who can guess what misery, how many lives lie buried there?

There is yet another mine not far from here - the Umba mine and Ivan takes me there. A long sloping corridor once led right into its bowels deep below the ground level, but not any longer, it has been bricked up. This mine was the thriving, vibrant heart of Revda in the 1960-70's; some 1,500 people worked here - half of the entire workforce in Revda. But then came Gorbachov and with him came market economy. The big Japanese machines pumping out the water seeping into the mine needed repairs and maintenance, but in Gorbachov Russia that was no longer financially viable... and Nature took its revenge! Ivan and I just stand there looking... and the rising water, having flooded the mine, now gushes out through what was once the entrance to the mine, and runs jauntily across the yard and the remaining few hundred yards on its way down to the river.

Ivan stands motionless and silent for a long moment. What emotions must have been pent up in his heart and mind - seven years of good work, good pay, camaraderie and life as one big family, canteen, social facilities, entertainment... all gone, all died from the "plague" of market economy. And Revda died with it too - no employment, no income... and his wife, he tells me, is recently out of work too!

The redundant Umba mine was acquired by an

enterprising woman from Murmansk for virtually nothing; now she is trying to sell it for an exorbitant price, but no one wants it. No, that's not true - human vultures want it. Only the carcass of the dead mine remains now - its doors and windows had long been taken, all its innards have gone too, the last remaining bits of steel and copper intestine are being stripped out, even external steel gantries are disappearing. Ivan walks me slowly through the mine; every part of this carcass is a part of him.

On the way back we travel sombre, in silence. Hesitatingly, I offer Ivan a 100 Rouble note and am surprised to see his face light up and smile in response – *how can anyone refuse money!*

Early next morning I am boarding a bus for Murmansk – Ivan is there and a number of other cars and drivers too, all touting for passengers, virtually pulling passengers off the bus... *four in a car, six in a van... cheap*! Hell, life must be tough in Revda. So, how could Ivan afford this Audi, I wonder? Is he perhaps yet another hapless part of a Mafia money-laundering scheme, even in a place as remote as Revda?

<u>Valley of Death, Valley of Tears - Murmansk</u>

"Valley of Death" or "Valley of Tears" in a place called Aleksandrov... It has to be here. Only nine kilometres from Murmansk, not far, yet no one here seems to know about it. But my father knew; 1,000 and possibly as many as 4,000 other Polish prisoners knew – their path led through this "Valley of Tears". There are formal testimonials to its existence by

Polish prisoners who were held there.

The Director of the Museum of Regional History in Murmansk is perplexed - Aleksandrovsk? The museum is truly impressive; you can see a huge print of Murmansk bombed and burnt out by the Germans, but *Aleksandrovsk... lagiers? Not around here... Yes, there is an Aleksandrovsk, and there might have been a GULAG lagier there, but that's a long way from here... Lagiers in, or within 9 km. of Murmansk? Peresylny lagier-346, or Punkt-55? No... I don't know about that.*

At my casual mention of "Memorial", the Director immediately puts me in touch with Irina, its representative. Irina is perplexed too... *a lagier 9 km. from Murmansk station?* I was hoping Irina would know; she represents the "Memorial" Foundation in Murmansk and has been fighting for the acknowledgement of the fate of the *represyonovany* people - the repressed, imprisoned, tortured, executed - in Soviet times.

Irina walks me along some of the main streets of Murmansk and points out buildings with some "history" behind them - that's where NKVD had their HQ, that's where so and so was imprisoned, executed... she knows these places well... she was the *Deputat* - Councillor - to the City of Murmansk for six years before she was ousted. It has been a hard fight but, finally, she has something to show for it in the main square, almost side by side with the official war memorial stands Irina's memorial to the

"VICTIMS OF POLITICAL REPRESSION"

The City had promised to fund a GULAG Museum in Murmansk, but they turned out to be empty promises and the project died. Has all knowledge of the *lagiers* died too; has the slate of history been wiped clean? But a number of official sources show a cluster of GULAG *lagiers* around Murmansk – but where, exactly, were they?

Yes, there is a *lagier,* a prison, in Murmansk, up on the hill, overlooking railway tracks and the northern end of the port - perhaps this is one of the GULAG *lagiers?* The light is fading but I want a photograph of the watchtower and barbed wire, and as the camera clicks, the guard in the tower spots me and sounds the alarm; immediately three guards rush towards me standing by the main gate… To forestall their wrath and possibly unpleasant consequences, I shout: *O.K, O.K… I have come all the way from England… my father was imprisoned here by the Soviets back in 1941… I want to show my grandchildren where it was…*

Perhaps taken aback by my frankness, the officer calms down and shouts: *no more photographs… get lost!* Of course I am happy to *"get lost"* now; I have a photo of the watch tower, the walls and barbed wire!

My frustration makes me take another look at the map of Murmansk published just this year, and there, to my amazement, marked in small but clear letters I see *"Dolyna Uyuta"* - "Valley of Homely Comfort "or "Valley of Welcome" – and, it lies exactly 9 km. north of the station on the main road; it can't be missed. It's there! I have found it! Just as it was described in the memoirs of those who had been imprisoned here: 9 km. from Murmansk, lying in the large rift in the granite rocks which fall away to the Bay of Murmansk to the west and swampy terrain to the east!

The Valley of Death and Tears has been renamed; it is now the "Valley of Homely Comfort" or the "Valley of Welcome"!

What strategy, what clever tactics; you have to congratulate 'Uncle' Stalin – no wonder he became Mr Churchill's and President Roosevelt's best friend-in-need and outwitted them at every step!

A steep descent leads to the base of the rift, now levelled, covered in tarmac, stocked with trees, walkways and benches. Indeed, it welcomes you now - come, sit, relax, read a book, look around… To the west - black rocks of granite; to the east – a high ridge opening onto flat, green terrain. I am standing on the floor of a natural amphitheatre. From up above, like in the Coliseum, the windows and balconies of modern blocks of apartments look down upon me; traffic and the populace on the high ground on the opposite side look down upon me trapped on the amphitheatre floor – I am nothing, count for nothing! What prisoner could have escaped from this kettle surrounded by natural walls of sheer rock topped with barbed wire? Here, the imprisoned Christians were not facing lions; here they were facing hunger, sickness and work beyond endurance; facing machineguns and the bayonets of the godless.
An elderly woman, neatly dressed, as if for some special occasion, was coming down the steps to the

floor of the amphitheatre. Oh yes, she is local, she has lived here from early childhood; no she doesn't remember any *lagiers* here... And Aleksandrovsk? *Why yes. Aleksandrovsk - that's right here; it's the old name of my town, now it's all part of Murmansk...*

Surely, this must be the place that Polish prisoners had written about in their memoirs, where my father might have been held – only the name has changed. "Valley of Welcome" - welcome indeed! I wonder what lies under the tarmac of this amphitheatre; there are no cemeteries in the neighbourhood, yet so many prisoners perished here. Who of the people sitting in the shade on the benches here, reading books, or basking in the autumnal sun knows who would have been sitting or standing, or dying right next to them back in 1941?

But the people of Murmansk have other very good reasons to remember 1941 and the War, and rightly so, for the town was completely destroyed and burnt out by German bombing; casualties must have been horrendous. The photographic mural in the Museum of Regional History shows Murmansk after the bombing – a shocking and unforgettable sight – nothing but rubble and skeletal remnants of buildings!

Today, Murmansk is impressive and its seaport extends several kilometres along the *Kolsky Zalyv*. On the highest point overlooking Murmansk, stands a huge statue of a soldier looking out west from whence the enemy came - not a particularly attractive statue, coarse and grey, but memorable for what it represents. This memorial, with its eternal flame and the magnificent view from this point over the city and the port, the open country melting into an infinite horizon, attracts many visitors and wedding parties. Until quite recently, one would have had to wade through scrub and bush to reach the memorial, but now, it's easily accessible by an asphalted road. The port presents a fascinating mass of infrastructure, ships and activity.

There were many more GULAG *lagiers* on the Kola Peninsula but who remembers them now – in Ponoi, Kandelaksha, Monchegorsk, Krasnoshelye, Kirovsk; and who knows where else. More and more lumber, quarries and railway tracks were required to support the war effort and the industrialization of the Soviet Union; more and more labour was needed for this task, and forced labour was easily acquired by the NKVD and supplied on demand.

A railway line was being built in the 1940's to link the mining sites at Revda, Apatity, Kirovsk, Oktyaberskoy, and a chain of labour camps was set up along the track in the direction of Krasnoshelye. Only vague memories of these GULAG camps remain now, and what is left of them is practically inaccessible by normal means of transport. Today they are remembered only as numbers – their distance from Oktyaberskoy: *62- km. 72-km. 82-km…*

The Ponoi *Lagier*

The welcoming party at the Ponoi *lagier* would not have been a surprise to any of the prisoners who found themselves transported here, not after the reception at the "Valley of Death", not any longer. And so it turned out to be. *Tut washa moghila* - proclaimed the camp commandant as they arrived at the *lagier* after their 'leisure' trip in the ship Staliniec. They understood; no need for translation; just look around; "this is your grave"… it is obvious.

That welcoming message - *tut washa moghila* - was to be implemented literally for the 3,500 prisoners from Juchnovo and Kozielsk disgorged here in May-June 1941; and so they were driven to work, exhausted and starving, to build a seaport, a military airfield and a road laid from local stone.

It was summer on Kola Peninsula but not a tree grew there, the sun burnt one moment, and next, the wind swept the open terrain or rain or sleet came to batter the emaciated prisoners. The ground remained frozen rock-hard just a foot or so below the surface, so what shelter could they have – cairns over pits into which they would crawl in twos to huddle together for warmth. But how long could they survive on a daily diet of 75 grams of bread (imagine - 75 grams!) and a little soup? They knew only a miracle could save them now.

And a miracle did happen. A "miracle" that all Polish prisoners had been praying for, for they knew it would be their only hope of salvation. On June 22, 1941, Hitler turned on his one-time friend - Stalin! War between Germany and Russia!

Within a week, or so, Finnish or German planes were

seen circling overhead; the prisoners waved their arms, threw their caps in the air, jumped... anything to attract attention to their plight. What was passing through their minds? Thank you Mr Hitler? How incredible, how perverse - but, right then, Hitler gave these men hope that they might escape certain death on the banks of River Ponoi.

By mid-July 1941, the next *etap* for them was ready. Many of the men from Ponoi were herded onto the ship "Uzbekistan". Conditions here were atrocious. Men were crammed into the holds below deck to an inconceivable extent: minimal food, minimal water, suffocating stench from the sweat and filth of men unwashed for weeks, of urine, of vomit and a lack of fresh air that came only from the gratings above... and they sat in the midst of it all four days on the White Sea before the boat arrived in Archangelsk!

July brought fine, warm weather and abundant greenery to Archangelsk, but for the men transported there from Ponoi, conditions were even worse; it was as if the slogan that greeted them in Ponoi was stuck on their backs in large capital letters - *Tut Washa Moghila*. Absolute starvation now; men refused to go out to work; NKVD brought out machine guns... but even that made no impact. For the men from Ponoi it was now all the same; better to die here, now, quickly.

But what of those left behind on Ponoi? And what of those men women and children from the depths of Poland on *etaps*, who continued to arrive in Ponoi? Military installations and the river port still had to be built; the airport still had to be built, the roads... the

Ponoi population continued to "flourish".

But *tut washa moghila* remained stuck to their backs, and neither time, nor rain, wind nor inhuman work could wash it off. And with the war won, and construction around Ponoi done, how could the NKVD dispose of 1000, 2000, and more, redundant human elements? Could 2000 or 1000, or even just a 100 graves be dug when the ground, even in summer, is still rock-solid a foot or two below the surface?

So where did the Polish men and women of Ponoi go? Yes... that's the question indigenous *Pomorcy*, I discovered, had been asking themselves as early as 1946. What happened to the Polish people that disappeared as suddenly as they had appeared? There were no investigative reporters then - not in Stalin's empire - but as recently as the late 1990's, there were men on Kola, still alive, haunted by these memories. War was still on in 1946 - cold war, even if no longer red-hot, and naval target practice was common on the White Sea - junk boats and redundant vessels were used for targets.

A naval rating sneaked onto the deck of his ship during a break in shooting; it was quiet, the sea calm... and somewhere, coming from the sea he could hear voices... men, women, crying out for help... it was eerie. He sneaked back; he now knew why he was not supposed to be on deck. Another witness will tell you: *we were towing out to sea a barge crammed with people. The barge was shot up for target practice... I cut the rope hauling the barge; it sank with all its prostitutes and criminals on board...*

Who of the Russian military, or the NKVD in 1946 would cry over the fate of these *"prostitutes and criminals"*? But, with the coming of Glasnost in the 1990's, men's consciences found a voice; stories began to circulate, and gradually, they were pieced together. These men now knew who the *"prostitutes and criminals"* were; and they knew now what happened to the Polish men and women prisoners on the Kola Peninsula… and now we know.

… … …

But I could be wrong thinking that my father was on Kola. Maybe he said Komi - not Kola; or what if he was taken east, beyond Arkhangelsk to eastern Siberia, or Workuta or Pechora, or even still further east on a journey-of-no-return to Magadan? The stories I have heard and read raise hair on my head.

Talk of Solzhenitsyn's Gulag Archipelago! Just listen to some fragments from Jan's story, a Polish officer and the father of a friend of mine. He survived the GULAG; he fought at Monte Cassino and lived to tell of the horrors of Stalin's evil empire.

"…one day they corralled us all and started calling out names: Polish, Russian, Uzbek and hard to tell what others. We were to get our things and line up by the gate; it looks like we are leaving Arkhangelsk….

It was a small ship; up the ladders onto the deck and down the ladders into the hold. In the middle of the ship, down inside the hold, timber staging from the floor all the way up to the deck securely isolated from the prisoners' section by strong decking. Above, on top - the guards, ship's crew and administration. Down below – massed human cattle. Nobody from the top deck would risk going down for fear of his life, so the criminals have free rein here. Fighting broke out to get better bunks or place. Everyone was eyed for what they may have of value: reasonable clothes, shoes and other useful things so that, in the dimmed lights at night, they can put a sharp knife to your throat and rob you in dead silence of everything they can sell on to others.

At first, the Poles put up with this but they finally had had enough; a group of young and strong Poles got together, tore staves and planks from the staging and made mince meat of the Muscovites. It was quiet after that except for minor flare-ups.

We were divided into groups, each with its own representative who collected our allocations of bread, fish and, sometimes, warm soup in a bucket. They supplied drinking water through a pipe from the top deck. One had to place cans, shells or even caps under the spout, and while your hands were raised to get water, thieves slipped their hands into your pockets and stole whatever was in them. That's how I lost my handkerchief – the last item I still had with me from Poland.

To get to the toilets, you had to go up some steps onto some kind of a half-deck and relieve yourself directly into the sea in the presence of an armed guard. There must have been some 2000 prisoners on board so the two available toilet seats couldn't cope even on the first day. If someone had bowel problems, he would need to visit the toilet more frequently, and after relieving himself, he would go back only to rejoin the end of the progressively longer queue. Already on the second day when we were on the open sea and the ship started rolling on the waves, the weaker of the men started suffering from seasickness and loose bowels. They couldn't wait for hours in the queue, so they squatted wherever they could and relieved themselves. At first it was into the fire buckets, then around them, and finally, just about anywhere.

On the half-deck at the level of the toilets, there was a small cabin, supposedly the sick room in case someone got sick. It had a metal floor with a hole in it and a bucket for flushing it down. Some of the more seriously sick prisoners, desperate from lack of help from the crew, broke down the door and occupied the cabin. I looked inside once. It was a horrible sight. Naked human skeletons filled the cabin. Some were lying on the floor, their bodies jerking in unison with the rolling of the ship, others sat or kneeled, yet others just stood there for lack of space holding onto the walls or the heads of others. They took off their clothes saturated with excrement and vomit and chucked them wherever. Some of the more conscious blocked their mouths and their rear with their hands to prevent total emptying of their gut but that didn't help much and strange-coloured liquids periodically spewed out of these outlets. Finally, exhausted in the extreme, oblivious to everything, they fell like dead wood on those already on the floor. It was some kind of an epidemic, "ponos" in their language. Maybe it was typhoid? Nobody from the guards showed up for fear of spreading this disease to the top deck even though the mound of skeletons grew progressively bigger.

Down below, prisoners started muttering, then shouting and finally hollering: "before we all die here we will sort you all out". The "authority" above seeing that they can't push them much further, got a number of Russian criminals, pumped them full of vodka and told them to clean up the sick room. These drunken criminals blocked access to the cabin and quickly cleaned it out. What they did – no one knows to this day. But there must have been at least fifty bodies inside, and half of them were still alive. They said they took them upstairs for treatment but no one saw the sick again. The sick room was on the same level as the half deck toilets and it had a window opening directly onto the sea.

The ship continued to roll in the sea. Not everyone had the strength or bothered to use the toilets or the sick room; they squatted wherever and relieved themselves through all three apertures simultaneously, for their mouths also took part in this. And with a thousand and more prisoners on board, the flat bottom of the ship was covered with a deep layer of slush of indescribable colour and killer stench. And when the ship dipped forward, this mass sloshed down towards the bow, and when the waves jerked the bow up, this whole mass bounced off the walls and sloshed backwards spraying excrement, bits of food and whatever else was in it onto the staging and their occupants. Our hands stank, our hair stank, wet clothes and shoes stank, everything stank, the whole ship stank. We were envious of cows that slept on dry straw; envious of pigs in the mire but it was their own. Your rags wet, face wet, wet hands giving out bread; you are starving but you can't eat this bread. Isn't it better to die rather than eat this bread soaked with excrement carrying some unknown disease.

The storm lasted three days – and we, down below, knew nothing about this – but apparently Moscow gave instructions to dump the human cargo with the disease into the sea but someone managed to persuade them that it's not so serious and eventually our ship reached the port after several days.

Was it a port – it's hard to say. The ship came as close as possible to the shore and we were told to jump into the water and wade to the shore. It wasn't deep and no one drowned, but it wasn't very courteous on the part of our hosts. The place was called "Narian Mar" at the mouth of river Pechora where a seaport was to be built. Sand, abundance of drinking water in the river Pechora and few armed guards – lifted our spirits. Who wanted to work could carry timber and boards and would then get better food rations. I couldn't, nor wanted to, so I got, like the others, only one slice of bread a day.

We stayed no longer than three days at this "resort". A boat, or perhaps a small ship came up to the shore and we were ordered, those of us who could still drag our feet, to get on, or into the boat. I thought it was a joke – the boat was full already and they were telling us, several hundred prisoners, to get on and kept on pushing us onto the boat. All the space on the benches is taken, space under the benches is taken, corridors are full, every little spot is taken, people sit on the floor and are happy to have found a place.

Full, full, brimming over. You want to go to the loo – only by stepping on their heads. You can't place a foot on the floor. The floor space is tightly packed and covered with human carcass. Some were still alive but pretended to be dead because that way they were not obliged to move to make space for others.

They gave us bread and salted fish and we continued up the river. All around us just scrub, water and forests. Perhaps once a day we see a shack covered with moss, two people dressed in rags standing on the bank of the river uncertain whether to waive the red flag in a welcome gesture, or what. Try to think – the brain refuses to work. What's going to happen to us; what's our fate – that's not important. The mind is fixated on only one thing - will they give us some bread today. But at least it was dry here, the floors were dry, adequate number of toilets, only getting to them was difficult because the boat was so tightly packed. Guards were nowhere to be seen; even one lifebelt was mounted high up on the stack so all could see. But most important of all, the air was fresh and clean, and the weather was fine and warm.

We entered river Pechora and went up to river Usa and continued up and up… Some days later, around noon, the boat docked and we were told to get off. This was Abis [Abez], the GULAG capital of Komi

Republic, 600 kilometres up the river, 7 kilometres inside the Arctic Circle, in the region of permafrost where the ground thaws to a depth of only half meter in summer. The lagier was named "Sievierno Żelazno Dorozhny Lagier". We were about a thousand.

A chunk of bread, a bowl of hot oatmeal soup and some rest improved our physical condition. Surrounded by armed guards and warned that they will shoot without warning anyone that steps to the left or to the right out of the column we marched out into the tundra…

Stunted forest, scrub and swamps surrounded us. We marched along a barely visible path in a sombre mood. We knew we were nearing our place of destination; we knew that it won't be a leisure camp for, up to now, no one has returned from the lagiers alive. We marched in silence, each of us in his own way scanning his past and what was dearest to him. We marched like robots…

… some of the guards were new but they should have been in our place. They were often brutal, even sadistic. If they thought someone wasn't working hard enough, they would make him strip naked and stand motionless, and suffer from the millions of mosquito bites and mites.

… in the autumn when milliards of these insect were about, it was impossible to work in the open. They gave us face nets and protective clothing, but even so, they would manage to get in and their bites were as if burnt by fire, the skin flared and itched until the following day.

… A naked man exposed for an hour to the bites of these mites, and particularly the huge mosquitoes in this region – would go mad from agony. He would shout, scream, moan and, forgetting that he may be shot for this, would run or roll on the ground as if wanting to bury himself in it.

… we had to clear the ground from peat accumulated over centuries. We were shown exactly what to do and how to achieve 120% of the daily norm. For that, you got 800grms. of bread, soup three times daily, main dish once, and the right to buy additional 200grms. of bread in the store – if you had money. For 100% of the norm you got 500grms. of bread and soup three times daily but that third bowl of soup didn't always materialize. Whoever did less than the norm was considered a "skiver" and got only 300grms. of bread and soup twice daily – morning and evening.

…I slowed down in the afternoon for it was obvious that I will in no way be able to do the norm. So, from after tomorrow 300grms. of bread and soup twice daily, and I will be labelled a "skiver". But who cares it's the stomach that counts.

Some physically stronger men beat the norms for shorter or longer periods, sometimes for weeks. They would eat well, to their full, but sooner or later they would strain their muscles and tear ligaments and suffer from unheard of cramps and pain, especially cramp in the arms. Both arms would suddenly turn inward and press with great force against the chest sending the man into deathly convulsions with guttural sound coming from his throat. If people were around, they could save him. One would hold his body down another would tear his arms away from the chest and straighten them out. The man would scream from agonizing pain, beg to be put out of his misery, but as blood started circulating again, he would recover.

…You are back in the camp now. Half a ladle of soup and you can go to sleep. But how can you fall asleep when you are acutely hungry; when for a smoke you would give half your soul away. So now you go hunting. You don't believe in luck but you have to try. You know you won't find any bread but maybe just one puff of cigarette. You are ready to ingratiate yourself, to do whatever it takes just for one puff. But bad luck. So you return to your place; you pray for a piece of bread, for quick death without those terrible cramps, for better life for your family, but your prayers are disturbed by another problem. Lice – unhappy with the poor nutritional quality of your blood bite deeper into your flesh looking for food. Sleep? How - when hundreds of lice are just waiting for that moment of peace? Kill them? How and when? Daytime you work. Night time, you shove your hand where it stings most but your fingers are stiff from work and cold. You can't feel the lice so you tear out a handful of hair with them and dump them onto the floor… What else can you do – eventually you fall asleep.

…An awful freeze, at least in our perception. Hard to

breath; the moisture in our breath freezes instantly into a mass of minute balls like lead shot for shooting birds. Hair, eyebrows, eyelashes, facial hair all covered with frost and adorned with icicles. Silence, not a breath of wind.

We are off for the night shift. It's not very dark for the Polar night illuminates the sky with lights as if taken from the "One Thousand and One Nights". What magnificent shapes, what magnificent colours, one can forever admire this spectacle of nature but…to be honest, I would rather lie on my bed of boards and gaze on the red-hot stove in our barrack.

How will I survive the next 12 hours until the morning? Will the warmth in my body last long enough? I ate my bread the moment it was handed out, that was in the morning. We got some soup in the evening but it was little more than hot water thickened with some flour. Where will I get the warmth and energy to last the night. A smoke would warm me and lift my spirits, but there's not a chance for even one puff throughout the night.

We are walking along a line of freight wagons. People are emptying the wagon. They work slowly, automatically; you can see they are exhausted, hardly able to move their arms and legs. Some have stopped work; they just stand there no longer able to unload the soil from the wagons of the train, which would then take them back to the lagier. In this freezing cold, to stand idle, leaning on your spade, that's almost certain death. Yes. Even before we reached the man leaning on the spade, the one next to him fell like a log. We ran up to him. Too late! He was frozen rigid. Even warm "holy water" wouldn't help him now. There were THREE such cases in just this brigade this night. And there were many nights like this one in the winter here; and many brigades...

...And now a new camp rule. Anyone who doesn't do the norm will remain in the place of work for an additional six hours and will return to the camp with the guard who delivers meals to his colleagues guarding us. And here the administrators made another mistake. Weak men would never do the norm, so if they were kept on site for an extra six hours, they would rapidly get weaker and weaker on their allowance of 100 grms. of bread. Within a day or two, three at most, he could no longer go out to work so they would take away his work boots and other rags and he would join the walking skeletons begging for scraps of food. There were more and more of these pitiful people with every day...

Sickness and disease finished men off. "Cynga" - the slow decay of flesh begun to spread; it was slow but progressive. "ponos" – infection of the bowels, constant diarrhoea sometimes with blood, as it was on the boat, made big dents in prisoner labour. It was reaching the scale of an epidemic. A man, exhausted and hungry, would run to the edge of the camp, sit on the wind-swept, ice-cold board encrusted with filth to relieve himself, then run back to the camp only to have to run back over and over again. He would soon lose all his strength and lie on his bed no longer able to move or care and relieve himself into his quilted trousers. No one cared, no one bothered him and he was soon dead. And on top of that, "opuchlizna" started spreading. First, the feet, then the legs would swell like logs, and when the swelling reached above the waistline, the man was ready. From the thousand, perhaps more, prisoners, about one third were unable to go out to work. Starvation and epidemics…

It was a desperate situation here. They cleaned out the camp from all seriously sick and completely isolated them, new cases of sick and exhausted men mounted daily. If they don't work, they lock them up in a cold, unheated barrack without any bedding or cover where they suffer severe frostbite to their hands and feet, where they get only 100grms. bread daily and stinking water. They don't go out to work because they can't. They lost all hope and faith; their spirit dead like their bodies…"[1]

What if my father had to survive a journey by sea and to such a place as Jan did? The thought makes me cringe, but it is a journey I will have to make... one day.

Clearing snow for rail tracks – 1940's

Across the taiga – 1940's

Building the railway line - 1940's

Abez (Abis) -transfer dock on river Usa 1940's

Abez (Abis) – construction of rail tracks - river Usa

Abez(Abis) - cemetery

Workuta coal mine 1940's

Workuta coal mine 1940's

Time off to study at the mines

A barrack in Workuta *lagier*

Workuta – the brick kilns (1960's)

Workuta – one of the cemeteries

Abez (Abis) – bridge over river Usa

Abez (Abis)– rail track, now removed, to river Usa

Uhta, Yarega – Domannik *lagier*

Yarega – deep mining of oil tars

6

Szli - do Armii... to join the Army!

Back in Murmansk - a wet mid-summer day: light drizzle from an overcast sky, the sea calm, the passenger terminal lifeless and silent... the quay deserted. Where are they all – the passengers, the workers, the crews? Has the memory of what happened seventy years ago made them run for cover in the basements of the terminal building? Are they still gripped by the fear of that moment in history, 22nd June 1941, when Hitler went for Stalin's throat? I have seen photographs of what Hitler did to Warsaw, and I have seen that huge photomontage in the museum here in town showing what Hitler did to Murmansk – nothing was left but rubble standing upon rubble! Frightening! Shocking what Man will do to Man!

I am alone on the quay, rainproof over my head. To my left, *"LENIN"* in white Cyrillic letters stigmatizes the coal-black hulk of the world's first nuclear powered icebreaker decommissioned and converted to a museum ship after two accidents in its reactor. To my right, *Kapitan Martyshkin* (built in Szczecin, Poland) a modern supply ship in flamboyant red waits to take men to the New World, or even further north to the forever-frozen land of Franc-Joseph, but thankfully, unlike in 1941, now it will bring them back. And right in front of me, the name of an elegant white passenger ship is disconcertingly staring me in the face... *Klawdiya Elinskaya... Klawdiya*

Elinskaya... Why! That's the ship that goes round the nose of the Kola Peninsula and calls at the small port at the mouth of river Ponoi! At the very place where the *lagier* was in 1942! It's due to sail the next day; the gangway was down; it was inviting me! Was it not for this reason that I came to Murmansk all the way from London to take this boat, to experience a sea voyage my father might have done in 1941? Yet, I stood there, transfixed! I didn't even make a move! Not one step to get on that boat! How can I explain it... if I don't understand it myself?

What held me back? Mental exhaustion from tramping in the land of Stalin's evil empire perhaps, or my own subconscious fear of the question gnawing my mind – what would I have DONE? What would I DO if I ever found myself on a boat, like the one Jan survived? Surely, in this state of mind it must be time for me to head back home to shore up my mental resilience and strength.

My tightly shut eyes began to leak tears of utter frustration and disbelief at this turn of events and shielded me from the reproach of the shocked taiga outside, but the wheels of my train taking me back home mercifully spun a somewhat kinder, more conciliatory message: *come-again... come-again... come-again...*

Yes... I will come again when I am stronger at heart and in spirit but, right now, I am holding a bunch of tickets in my hand - St Petersburg, Moscow, Minsk, Warsaw, and London... an infinite distance from here, but home.

London? How strange, how curious… I came here all the way from London to find traces of what fate had ordained for my father in those years of War… but why from London? Why not from Wielowieś or Postawy, from the Homeland my father and hundreds of thousands of Polish people had suffered for, fought for, died for?

What made him choose life in exile? I should have asked, but I didn't, and now only very hazy fragments resurface in my memory: me, a small boy of perhaps six… great commotion in the Polish camp in Valivade in India… some men and women came to the camp… there was talk of return to Poland… great anger in the camp… my mother angry too… no, no, no… nobody's going back to Poland; never again will we live under a communist regime. Thank the Lord we got out!

Yes… I should have asked but I was happy living in the land of his exile, oblivious of the causes or reasons. But before setting out on this journey, I posted a question on the Forum of the "Kresy-Siberia Foundation" many members of which are essentially of the same background as mine - the second and third generation descendants of Polish men and women who chose exile after the War. My question was simple: "Odyssey Abandoned – Why?"

And as the wheels of my train go round and round, taking me home, I have time to dwell on their responses.

… … …

"To: JK (the author) From: JP (War veteran)
Subject: Odyssey Abandoned - Why?

The word "Abandoned" is harsh, insulting and is intended to show a total disregard for something. (Some definitions for abandon: Deserted, Discarded, Forsaken, Derelict, Vacant, Dumped, Neglected, Cast off, Ditch). None have a pleasant connotation. None should be used to describe the Polish people regardless where they reside or why they reside there.

How would he feel if the word was used to describe why he abandoned his buddy on the battlefield when all he did was to get help or medical supplies for his wounded buddy?

The same holds true for us. There is absolutely no reason for the Polish people especially the Polish refugees to defend their historical actions regarding their life or their family's reasons to or not to return to Poland.

It breaks my heart when Poles have to respond by trying to justify their actions to these types of demeaning statements or questions, like why did you or your family abandon Poland?

Polish people especially the Polish refugees need to over and over tell of their glorious, brave and suffering history but not because they have to defend their actions because of insulting questions but only to tell the truth or just as a fact of one's personal experience and let the chips fall where they may…"

"To: JP From: M
Subject: Odyssey Abandoned - Why?

I am deeply moved by your post. You captured the essence of the Polish drama. What pains me greatly is the lack of understanding of the

Sybiraki (Polish people deported by Stalin to Siberia now living in self-imposed exile) situation in Poland.

This topic was suppressed and forbidden for 50 years and not much has been done in the past 20 years of independence to educate the Polish public about the fate of millions of Polish citizens who found themselves in the West after the war.

Apart from the communist propaganda that still reverberates in the minds of the Polish people not even a comprehensive study has been undertaken by the Polish government on the Polish people who did not return to Soviet controlled Poland after the war. As with the Polish people left behind in the Soviet Union, Poland to this day is not looking after its own people as much as other countries do, and as much as the unique situation of the Polish people would require.

The Polish communist government, the so called PRL, often treated the Poles abroad as political enemies. That attitude has not changed as much as it should after 1990. The lack of strong leadership on this issue from Warsaw results in reckless questions like the one that caused you and other Sybiraki much pain, and rightfully so. There is so much to do to remedy this situation but so little has been done thus far..."

"To: Group From: R
Subject: Odyssey Abandoned - Why?

After some thinking I came to the conclusion that perhaps the question was not intended to "insult" anybody but was put on the table just to find out why so many Poles did not go back to Poland after the WWII. The following is an attempt to clarify this.

To begin let me say that the decision of staying in the West for us, Polish veterans, is a very touchy subject. You have to understand that at that time, communist press in the West and in Poland was proclaiming that we were traitors, we did not want to go to Poland as good Polish patriots, where we were needed to rebuild "strong Poland united in the brotherhood with our great friend Soviet Russia who gave us freedom from the yoke of the Nazis". The propaganda from Warsaw called us opportunists who elected to have a cosy life of capitalists rather than follow our duty to go to work for Poland.

And to the British we were "Bloody Foreigners". Well, it was not so easy to stay in the West. We did not know the language. The opportunities were limited. The jobs that were available were domestic help, washing dishes at the Lyon's Restaurants or coal mining. Some emigrated to Canada, Australia or Argentina and started their lives there under very harsh conditions. To find your place in the society and get some education was very difficult....

We did not stay in the West to enjoy an easy life. Our hearts were out there - in Poland. But we did not have a choice: it was either go back, submit to the regime that we hated, that was imposed on our country, or try to find a place in the world here. I know that for some of my friends the decision was very difficult and I understand that in many cases they did not have any other choice but to go back. There were many families that did not survive this difficult time. In my case the decision was rather easy to take. Out of four brothers three of us were in the West and my parents, who were also deported, were too. For many it was much more difficult. But that was war…"

"To: JK From: Z
Subject: Odyssey Abandoned - Why?

There is nothing wrong with being passionate and an idealist! I did not find your question to be insulting, in fact I welcomed it. I thank you because it made me take stock of my standpoint.

When I visited Poland a couple of years ago I was struck by its homogeny. The goods available in the shopping malls were exactly the same type as in England, France, Belgium, Germany and Lithuania. The people dressed generally the same, drove similar cars, worked in generally the same areas of expertise. They were as friendly, arrogant, drunken, polite, brash, uncouth and vulgar as in any other country I have spent time in. The same urban degradation such as graffiti, smashed windows and litter was apparent. The only way to differentiate in which country I found myself was to actually listen to the predominant language spoken around me or drop into an antiques store.

For me, the Poland of my parents is long gone and will never return. They knew it and accepted their lot for the sake of my sister and I and I am pretty certain that they would have been both horrified and terrified, yet proud, if either of us had shown any inclination to live in Poland. The political climate in Europe is completely different to that of 75 years ago. Any rabid nationalism is generally contained albeit still simmering away, communism has been all but wiped out. Consumerism rules! Anti-Polonism exists in Lithuania and Belarus but people aren't being deported or gaoled just for being Polish, although they do perceive that they experience disadvantages....

The question that begs to be asked is: is it fair and proper for a nation to expect its permanent residents to take on citizenship of that country?

I cannot speak with any formal authority but what I have seen here in my country of choice is that Australia has a tradition of welcoming migrants from all over the world and yes, picking on them! In the 1950's and 60's it was the Greeks, Italians and Lebanese. The 1980's saw the Vietnamese and Cambodians, the last 2 decades of the century saw a relaxation of immigration rules and an influx migrants from all over the world....

Do all these migrants feel they have abandoned their country of origin? Probably they all feel that to a greater or lesser degree. Should we folk of Polish heritage feel the same way? That is an individual choice but I feel that if an individual cannot, with hand on heart, answer "Yes" to the question of citizenship, then that individual should seek residence in the country to which they feel most attached...".[2]

A number of comments came from the younger generation. For them, like for my own children and grandchildren, there is no issue - they were born, grew up and grew old in the country of their parents' exile, their children were born there too... went to school, lived a normal life; for them there was no 'Odyssey', their loyalties were clear, their heart and mind belonged to the country of their birth - be it the USA, Canada, Australia or Brazil...

But for my father, that welcoming message at the Ponoi *lagier* - *tut washa moghila* - this is your grave - must have remained forever in his mind; he would never voluntarily return to his Homeland while the same NKVD oppressors worked hand in hand with their Polish partners - the UB (Internal Security) and UOP (National Security Bureau). Return to Poland at that time would have meant prison for him and persecution for his family. No, he would rather live in exile with his family. In Great Britain he carried an altogether different welcoming message on the back of his coat: W.C. FRENCH, the name of a building contractor, and it spelt employment, food, freedom, life... No, he would never go back while Communism ruled in his Homeland.

For my father, and the thousands of others who had tasted death in the GULAG *lagiers* and found salvation and honour in the Anders Army, life gave a bitter lesson, but the British welcoming message must have given my father hope and opened the door to a new life and a more secure future for his family.

Regrettably, my father died long before Poland became free as it is today. He never spoke of an "Odyssey" and yet, in my heart, I feel that he left it un-said, that he wished in his "un-spoken will" that his son will one day complete the Odyssey, and return to a free and independent Poland. And at a moment like this on the train home from Murmansk I feel suspended in the deep fissure created by the War...

my right elbow resting on Postawy, now in Belarus, where I was born but know not, and my left elbow resting on England where I was not born but know, where I grew up and grew old, and where my children and their children live: in England, in their Homeland.

And at this moment of black introspection, I reach for my "pocket bible" better known as *"Piosenki z Plecaka Helenki"* [Songs in Helen's Backpack] by Feliks Konarski/Ref Ren/[3] A small book, brown with age and wear, written and published by "Ref Ren" in 1946 - a compilation of his songs, music scores, sketches and cabaret humour to entertain and uplift the spirit of Polish soldiers in the Ander's Army on their long march from the depths of Stalin's empire to their exile in England - their "Odyssey".

Flick gently through its pages and you feel that yearning of every man and woman soldier for their Homeland, for Lwów, for Wilno, Warsaw… for every handful of Polish soil wherever that might be; you feel their determination to fight, their readiness to lay down their lives for Poland, for freedom… to return home! And so they "walked"… and somewhere amongst them would have "walked" my father.

> *"Szli*
> *Z twarzami szarymi, jak popiół…*
> *Z oczyma zapatrzonymi w przyszłość…*
> *Każdy z nich bólem się opił,*
> *Każdy cierpieniem nakarmił…*
> *Szli*
> *Do Armii…!*
> *W zawszonych łachmanach*

Z nogami, owiniętymi w szmaty…
Pod niejednym ugięły się kolana
Niejednemu zdrętwiały gnaty
I zęby szczękały z mrozu…
Szli
Z odległyvh kołchozów,
Z zatłoczonych, ponurych miast,
Nie widząc słońca i gwiazd,
Nie słysząc wichru złośliwego wycia,
Zmęczeni, głodni, bez życia,
Ale uparci, ale wierzący
W prawość Tej, której na imię: Polska!
Szli
Do wojska!" (p.46)

[They walked
With faces grey, as cinders…/ With eyes focused on future…/All brim-full with pain,/All satiated with suffering…
They walked
To join the Army…!
In attire full of lice,/ Legs wrapped in rugs…/ On quaky knees,/ Numbness in their limbs/ Teeth chattering from cold… They walked
From faraway kolkhozes,/ From grim and crowded towns,/ Seeing neither sun nor stars,/ Not hearing the howling of wind,/ Tired, hungry, lifeless,/ But determined, but convinced/ Of the right of the One, who's name is: Poland!
They walked
To join the Army]

And indeed, like the wheels of my train today, all rail tracks, roads, paths, tracks, rivers and streams throughout "Stalin's Evil Empire" in 1941-2 led Polish people to Buzuluk, Tockoye, Tatishchevo… to the Anders Army.

"*Szli*" – how can I express this monosyllabic word in Engish; how can I translate the misery and the determination of people to escape from Stalin's "Garden of Eden" in the middle of Siberian winter, in a world submerged in snow, in cutting blizzards, temperatures in the -40's and -50's, on foot, dragging sledges across the snow-bound wild taiga? Fathers, mothers, grandparents, children and babies swathed in rugs… dying from exhaustion along the way, yet still they "walk". Men and women old, young and under-aged dreaming of joining the Army, determined to fight again, yearning to return home? The word "walk" or "trek" is so inadequate.

And somewhere, amongst these thousands, was my father; walking to the nearest railway station… to join the Army!

> *Coś ty za jeden, przyjacielu mój,*
> *Że masz na sobie taki dziwny strój?*
> *Jam z niwoli polski żołnierz,*
> *Został mi z munduru kołnierz*
> *I podszyty wiatrem płaszcz..!*
> *Cóż za łachmany ty na sobie masz*
> *I taką dziwną wynędzniałom twarz?* (p.12)

[Who are you my dear friend,
Attired in such a strange garb?
I'm a Polish soldier returning from captivity.
All I have now is this collar from my uniform

And my coat lined with wind!
Why such rags
And such gaunt face?]

And then my "pocket bible" flips open on page 5.

"24th December 1941, a train packed full pulled up at a small, snowed-in railway station, although no different from so many other Soviet stations, it entered the annals of history, Polish History. The station was called: Tockoye.

"That day, I saw for the first time – with the dilapidated building and its equally scruffy, happy residents in the background – a genuine Polish policeman wearing an English cap and a much too-long trench coat with shiny brass buttons."

"…I saw that buttoned-up army coat and the buckled-up shiny lather belt. It's that leather belt that moved me so much as memories of that sunny day in September floated in front of my eyes, when large groups of disarmed soldiers, without belts, roamed the streets of Lwów gripped by fear. A frightful day…"

"At a small railway station stood a soldier in full military gear and buckled up belt..! So the fight isn't over yet! So the calamity of September was only a battle lost… the War is not lost…"

"In a war where the highest principles are at stake: the freedom of Poland and the civilized world! One has to fight, and if a battle is lost, one has to rise to fight again!"

And that policeman! In the English uniform… only a cap in place of the black beret! He could so easily have been my father. I can hear his voice amongst the thousands!

> *"Myśmy w obronie wolnośći*
> *Pierwsi ruszyli na zew!*
> *Myśmy dla szczęścia ludzkości*
> *Pierwsi przelali swą krew!" (Song No.1)*

[We in defence of freedom / Were first to answer the call! / We for the happiness of peoples / Were first to shed our blood!]

No! They walked though starving, cold, exhausted... but still they walked to the very end! No! I can't go home, not yet, not now!

And so... the wheels of my train must go on, and on, and on... but on a different track - an old and well worn railway line: Leningrad, Moscow, Saratov, Kuybyshev, Tockoye, Buzuluk, Tatischevo...

Tockoye

Tockoye! A young soldier on sentry duty... in khaki and a cap on his head! Thin, obviously hungry... but he's not Polish! He's Russian! Still, he looks at my passport, listens to my story, calls the guard-house... the guard calls the commanding officer and... Yes! Leave my passport, and I am allowed to walk up to the bridge on the river – their military base is on the other side.

How strange, naïve perhaps... but I feel disappointed. I would so much like to see and feel the way it was back in December 1941 when my father might have been here; to see and feel as "Ref Ren" did at the time – snow-covered open steppes as far as the eye can see, row upon row of tents sitting deep in snow… groups of men still hungry, still in rags, freezing, walking the four kilometres through deep slush from Tockoye station to the Polish army camp across the bridge I am standing on right now, the river frozen solid… But of course, I am seventy years too late to share their history with them. It's May, the sun shines, perfect summer weather…

My Russian soldier in khaki on sentry duty is bored, he has no higher motives… a smoke and vodka will see him through the eighteen months of military service. But even in times of such peaceful ambience as today, not every soldier survives – three young Russian men with happy smiling faces look up at me from the roadside marker some two hundred metres from the sentry; three Orthodox crosses next to their faces tell their story. Were they, or was it the driver of the vehicle that killed them, drunk on the way to or back from Tockoye station? A little further along, in a depression in the surrounding fields sits a squadron of tanks; men cook lunch near-by… Tanks! And our "soldiers" didn't even have rifles at the time, not even boots!

A man in a 4x4 BMW gives me a lift back to the station… Oh yes! He knows about Polish soldiers. In fact, commemorative celebrations of these events were held in Tockoye in 2011; many of the old folks still remember how good and helpful the Poles were and how sad they all were to see them go, for they showed the Russians that it is possible to be human in a free-er world.

Tockoye - still very much a *"small railway station... no different from so many other Soviet stations..."* It's a miserable little station with a large single-story hall and little else; only a white bust of Lenin in front of the station reminds people of its history, and a black tablet commemorates its birth:

STATION
TOCKAYA
BUILT
1877

I hail a private car in the street and the driver gives me a lift to Buzuluk. Inevitably, its two young passengers, the driver and I exchange the "why-s and where-s" and at the mention of Anders all three come to life – of course they know about the Poles, about Anders, about the Army in Buzuluk! In fact, they tell me, there's a commemorative plaque on the wall of the Army HQ building. Of course they will take me to my hotel, no problem at all and absolutely no payment due for the ride!

Buzuluk

And so I search for that commemorative plaque… in a lovely small town bathing in warm sunlight today. This garrison town with its history dating from 1736 has been scarcely touched by War, and a number of solid red brick buildings impress with their architecture as do several exquisite log and timber houses from the early 20th. Century. Almost wherever you look a plaque commemorates its history and its place in the War of 1941-1945, yet no one I met in the street could tell me where the Anders Army HQ stood, but a black plaque on the wall of the railway station remembers:

30 JANUARY 1943
DEPARTED FOR THE FRONT
1ST INDEPENDENT
CZECHOSLOVAK
BATTALION
RAISED IN BUZULUK
IN 1942-1943

Indeed, that's exactly what Stalin had in mind for the Anders Army too - disperse Polish battalions in the mass of the Red Army; send them now, no matter that they are barely out of the GULAG and had inadequate training... for even in their present pitiful condition they were more than good-enough to stop German bullets. Thankfully, General Anders knew well Stalin's mentality, and saved his Army!

Eventually and almost by accident, I come upon an impressive white building... silence, only one or two people in sight, but the grey plaque I was looking for is there.

W TYM BUDYNKU
W OKRESIE IX 1941 - 1942
MIEŚCIŁO SIĘ DOWÓDZTWO I SZTAB
ARMII POLSKIEJ W ZSSR
FORMOWANEJ PRZEZ GENERAŁA
WŁADYSŁAWA ANDERSA

[The HQ and the General Staff of the Polish Army in the USSR formed by General Władysław Anders was based in this building from IX 1941 – I 1942]

In that winter of 1941-2 their entire world was snowed in, howling winds and temperatures in the -40's, yet still they walked - to join the Army! Yet still, they…

*"Szli
Do wojska!"*

A long, long queue waited outside the Army reception centre… Weak, sick, but their spirit high, they all wanted to enlist in the Anders Army; they all wanted to fight the Germans. Their hopes were high; there… in the future, glimmered a free and independent Poland. Somewhere in that queue surely would have stood my father.

But how would I know him – I was only six months old when he left. Would his own wife recognize him after what he had gone through? And would he recognise his own wife and children after what they had gone through during their two years in Stalin's "Garden of Eden" in the wild steppes of Kazakhstan?

One by one the men in that long queue gave their name, their date and place of birth, their rank, and wrote down their story; and one by one these stories become a litany of woe and of inhumanity of Man to Man in Stalin's empire - in Murmansk, Arkhangelsk, Workuta, Ukhta, Abez and GULAG *lagiers* in Kazakhstan and at "the end of the world" as far away and as remote as Kolyma. But as they came up one by one, their eyes shone with the will to fight and to lay down their lives for Poland if need be.

And seventy years later, as I leaf through their testimonials, shivers run up my spine for somewhere in that maze of *lagiers* was my father... and this thought, and one awful question gnaws my mind: what would I have done if I had ever found myself where they had been, if I ever had to take the test my father and so many others had to take... What would I do:

- when facing death from starvation would I snatch an inmate's feeding bowl... or share my last crumbs with him?
- and when hunger drove me crazy would I resist NKVD's solicitations to tell on other prisoners, or become a *stahanowiec*, to get a little more food... so I can live a little longer?
- or when my old and utterly exhausted father fell by the wayside, for he could walk no further, would I cradle him in my arms and wait for that final bullet... or would I find an overriding reason to abandon him... to walk on... to stay alive?
- and when a *zhulik*, bent on stealing my last crumbs of bread, threatens me with a knife would I meekly yield, call for help, or fight?
- And when I see my mates being torn to shreds or pulped into a bloody mash in those merciless battles for Monte Cassino... would I cower, or kill?

By whichever route his fate took him, my father survived; he made it to Buzuluk and enlisted with the Anders Army. For him and some 115,000 Polish people, Buzuluk became the end of their GULAG

Trail; it was also their first step on their trail to exile. On the way they would first have to pass some bitter milestones: the abandonment at Tehran, the perfidy at Yalta, the infamy of Katyń, the sacrifice on the battlefields in Italy, and the perversity on Victory Day in London... all shrouded in the fog of political expediency.

But for so many of those who "*Szli*" to join the Anders Army, the end of the GULAG trail became the end of their life's trail; they stayed behind forever... in their graves even at the very exit from "Stalin's Evil Empire". So many could not shake off Stalin's evil spell - *tut washa moghila* - and succumbed to exhaustion and sickness - to typhoid, scarlet fever, malaria... and Polish graves in their hundreds fill cemeteries in Kazakhstan, Turkistan, and in Bukhara, Ghuzar, Kanimekh, Kermine and so many other places in Uzbekistan.

7
Deliverance… or Death?

"…We had just started out on our trek to the new camp when a truck full of Russian soldiers waving flags and shouting passed us…. What? What are they shouting…? "WSIE POLAKI AMNESTIROVANI" "DOHOVOR SIKORSKI – MAJSKI". Polish prisoners are now Stalin's greatest friends! We will be freed from the GULAG lagiers to enrol in armed forces; free to fight the Germans - now our common enemy. "Wsie Polaki amnestirowani… Wsie Polaki amne… Amnesty for all Poles… "Sikorski-Majski Understanding… the truck sped on.

Did we hear right..?
Did we understand it right..?
Can this be true..?" [4]

Where was my father at the time of that "miracle" all Polish prisoners had been "praying" for? What passed through his mind when he heard those words in Jan's story: *"Wsie Polaki Amnestirovani", "Dohovor Sikorski – Majski"…* when he saw Soviet armed guards waving flags, smiling… The NKVD ready to shake hands! Amnesty for all Poles? Jubilation, disbelief, suspicion?

How could anyone believe the Soviets… that he and others will be freed to sign up for military service - with Polish armed forces? Believe the NKVD? Believe the accuser, torturer, the executioner? Surely they have already suffered so much at the hands of the Soviets - their lies, propaganda, perversity, duplicity … is this not perhaps yet another Soviet trick to identify those that might have had such notions in their heads? But if war with Germany had, in fact, erupted… "my enemy's enemy now becomes my greatest friend" and could Hitler have a greater enemy now than the Poles?

And indeed, on 30th July 1941 an understanding, known as the Sikorski-Majski Agreement, was signed by Soviet Russia and the Polish Government in Exile in London. It envisaged the formation of a Polish army on Russian soil to fight the now common enemy - Hitler's Germany! Incredible, amazing news and fresh hope of deliverance from Stalin's hands for thousands of Polish men, women and children held in prisons and labour camps throughout Russia, Kazakhstan and other Republics in the south and east of Stalin's empire. Polish people have found their Moses! General Władysław Sikorski was to lead them out of the land of the Soviets to a free and independent Poland - if only Biblical history would repeat itself - and General Anders was to lead the Army.

Imagine the utter consternation, disbelief and confusion amongst the NKVD in the GULAG system? Could an NKVD officer, brainwashed to despise these "prostitutes, criminals, enemies of the people, traitors…" having been made the master of their life and death, suddenly, from one day to the next, see them as friends and allies? Many couldn't and didn't, and many Poles held by NKVD didn't hear about the "Amnesty" until too late, and even if they did, the NKVD would find reasons to hold them in the GULAG system.

Thankfully, in Arkhangelsk as in other GULAG lagiers the NKVD relented; machineguns didn't fire on *refusnik* Polish prisoners. Instead, men were again herded into freight wagons and the *echelon* went south. But conditions here were even more atrocious. Hunger, heat and, above all, thirst drove men mad - only fresh hope of deliverance with the Anders Army kept them alive.

From the remotest regions of Stalin's empire all roads now led to Buzuluk, Tatischevo, Totskoye... to the Polish Army, to renewed hope, or be it death in their fight to free Poland from German occupation. But thousands of men, women and children couldn't shake off their fate - *tut washa moghila* – and died of cold, starvation, sickness, physical exhaustion; they found their final resting place in the bleakness of the tundra, or taiga, or... along the railway tracks.

... ...

Rat tat tat... rat tat tat... rat tat tat... No, no... it's not machinegun fire - too regular for that - it's the wheels of a train coming into a station...

As an *echelon* from Archangelsk *"packed full pulled up at a small, snowed-in railway station, although no different from so many other Soviet stations"*[5] the moment the rattle of wagon wheels on the rails died down a new sound erupted: *wody, wody, pić...* water, water, drink; several arms sneaked out waving through the grills of the windows. The large crowd sitting on their packs along the platform fell silent, listened and, suddenly, became electrified... *to Polacy, Polacy... nasi chłopcy*. Look...

Look... Poles, Poles, our men! Many got up, filled whatever containers they had with water and rushed towards the outstretched arms, but the soldiers beat them back; other soldiers mounted the roofs of the wagons and started banging on them to quell the intensifying cries for help.[6]

An old woman, oblivious of the risk, somehow got through the line of soldiers and walked slowly towards an outstretched hand... *stop, get back... or I shoot...* As she lifted a can towards the outstretched hand a shot rang out... her knees buckled and she fell to the ground; the water spilt, but not enough to wash the blood off the stones. The crowd fell silent and looked on in horror... what can they do... what can they do?

What drove that old woman to certain death? Didn't she hear the warning? Was it perhaps the thought of her son being amongst those *nasi chłopcy* - our men? Was it courage like that of a soldier on the battlefield carrying his wounded comrade back into safety; was she simply a "deaf old hag" as the soldier who fired the shot would have said?

The train slowly pulled out of the station. In silence, the crowd settled back on their packs but a boy remained standing as if transfixed by the shooting of the old woman; hands limply along his side, eyes glazed with tears... that hand begging for water – was it not perhaps his father's? And that old woman... only yesterday, he buried his own grandmother... He just stood there, waiting... along with a thousand or more Polish soldiers, men, women, children... No, not this train! Perhaps the next... or the next... will take him to Buzuluk.

Perhaps fourteen or fifteen - old enough to remember - he could tell you a story not unlike that of tens of thousands of others children. His father, as mine, said goodbye at the end of August 1939, but his father, unlike mine, was never to be seen or heard from again.

In April 1940, as in my case, the boy, with his mother, brother and his grandmother, had been deported from their home in Poland to find themselves in a forsaken *kolkhoz* in the depths of Russian taiga. Here he had to learn fast the first commandment: *ne rabotayet ne kushayet* – you don't work, you don't eat - equally applicable to all. And what work was there for a young boy, his mother and his aged grandmother... in a logging camp, in the remotest part of the taiga! He had seen death from starvation, from freezing cold, from sickness, accidents at work... yet such wanton destruction of human life as he had just witnessed, he had never seen.

But fate favoured the boy; he found his way to Buzuluk and joined the Army Cadets. After the war, he came to England and, as my father and our family, he made London his home. Indeed, the boy was fortunate, for so many along the GULAG trail perished even at the very exit from "Stalin's Evil Empire". So many died from plagues of typhoid, scarlet fever, dysentery, malaria... and Polish graves in their hundreds fill cemeteries in Kazakhstan and Uzbekistan.

8

Exit by the cemetery

Szli...
...Szli
Szli...

And they kept coming... to join the Army. But their dream Army could only take those that had a fair chance of recovering from their two years in Stalin's *lagiers*. Many of those that reached Buzuluk, Tockoye and Tatischevo, were old, sick, weak, half-starved people exhausted by the ordeal of their trek, and they had only a small chance of surviving the harsh Russian winter. The number of food rations allocated to the Army by the NKVD was woefully inadequate; the only shelter from the elements the Army could find were tents sitting in deep snow, and a few draughty shacks and *zemlankas*; hospitals were inadequately equipped to deal with the outbreaks of contagious diseases, and lacked sufficient medicines to deal with them - a desperate and heart-breaking situation.

A Polish Army of 90,000 men under General Anders was to be formed on Russian soil to fight the German foe. Stalin, now an ally of the Polish government in exile, would have happily thrown the Anders Army, just as it stood, to fight the Germans – Poles will do to stop German bullets! But when General Sikorski and Anders resisted, Stalin cut the number of army rations from 90,000 to 40,000!

The words of General Anders, *"We have to forget past*

injustices… and fight to the end the common enemy, Hitler, at the side of our Allies, at the side of the Red Army." began to ring hollow in this situation. Yet still they came - the Army and General Anders was their only hope - my father's only hope too, and my family's only way to salvation.

Under great pressure from General Sikorski, General Anders and the Allies, Stalin relented and in return for a big reduction in the number of rations he agreed to the relocation of the Polish Army to his southern Republics. There, the climate was warm and the land, if not quite "flowing with milk and honey", held out a promise of peaches, grapes, strawberries and cream - if only it were so.

The Army H.Q. moved to YangiYul near Tashkent in January 1942, and now all trains from all over Stalin's empire taking the "amnestied" Polish people to the Army were directed southeast - Kuybeshev, Buzuluk, Tockoye, Chkalov, Aralsk by the Aral Sea, Qizil Orda, Turkistan and Chimkent in Kazakhstan… to Tashkent and YnagiYul, and other places in Uzbekistan, Turkistan, Tajikistan, Kyrgyzstan and even further south.

The threat from machineguns had gone, but the misery of the men, women and children seeking salvation continued; hunger and severe cold in winter, and Stalin's total contempt for human life took a heavy toll. The first echelon of some 600 people at risk from the severe Russian winter of 1940-41 sent south to Tashkent turned out to be an unforgiveable disaster. Men, women and children weakened to the extreme by the lack of provisions for this long train journey were dispersed amongst the local *kolkhoze*s themselves suffering from near starvation and lack of shelter - only one or two from this echelon managed to get back to Buzuluk to tell their story of woe.

....

And seventy years later the wheels of my train go on and on and on... for 3,400 kilometres following their trail from Moscow to Tashkent. Would I dare travel 1st or 2rd class with the misery of the amnestied people foremost in my mind? It's the *platz-card* for me, the cheapest places in the 3rd or 4th class wagons – a reserved seat on a padded bench that converts into a sleeping bunk!

Show your ticket and your passport to the "boss" of the wagon, climb up the three metal rungs and you enter – Hell! How can I get to my seat #56 at the far end of the wagon through this bedlam! Talk of obesity? Here it's normality! Women twice or more my size and strong enough to squelch me out of their way or push me out through the window! Big, strong men too, doubling in size by the amount of luggage and packs around them! The few slim men and women look impoverished, miserable and belch cigarette smoke; and all, like me, are forcing the narrow corridor to their assigned *platz*.

One minute, five, ten, twenty... the visitors leave, the bye byes done, the train jerks, the wheels begin to turn and... unbelievably, the bedlam subsides. Now you can see a long row of small cells - three bunks stacked on each wall of each cell, a small table fits tightly between the two stacks, one window with a metal bar across, no door onto the corridor so the "boss" can keep an eye on you... three more bunks stacked along the window on the other side of the corridor... What is this - a modern version of the old *Stolypin* wagon?

At last, now you can relax, look at thy neighbour, spread a tablecloth and set your food on the table; no shortage of *kipiatok* from the coal-fired *samovar* at one end of the wagon. There's room for me too, but my tomato, cucumber and bread look somewhat embarrassing next to my neighbours' sausage, *slonina,* hard-boiled eggs, noodle soups, bread, butter, fruit & veg, soft drinks now mounting on the table. Only vodka is missing – no alcohol allowed on trains in Russia and in Kazakhstan... and in theory!

For a few Roubles more, the "boss' gives out fresh bed linen and an extra blanket if you need one, and everybody is soon getting ready for the "first night". But get up in the night, take a step or two towards the WC, and your mind convulses – you are still alive and awake... but in a morgue! Cadavers lie under white sheets, all neatly stowed on shelves, feet sticking out, into the corridor, heads invisible in the murky light; silence... no, not quite, the body nearest you is still breathing; you are still holding your breath!

But with the sunrise, the morgue comes to life as does the warmth, generosity and good humour of the Russian people... and passport control. A blond and rather good looking young woman toting a pistol at her side takes my passport, looks at me and with a laugh calls over her superior... *hey, what kind of a passport is this, never seen it before*! Everyone looks in my direction - what's this, who's he, will they lead him away? *This is an English Passport; there, see, it says - Wielika Britania* – lectures a man of the world... that's why he is her superior.

Ah... a man from England! Come, join us, share our breakfast, lunch, supper... tell us how it is in England, how much does it cost, what do I do, how much do I earn, can I live on my pension – *we can't, we have to "improvise" as best we can*; have I got photographs... am I married, any children, how long - *what!? Forty years married to the same woman? Wow! I am forty and I have been married four times – that's quite normal in Russia* - a still quite pretty forty-year-old woman tells me.

A couple of seats further down the corridor an old man and his wife sit quietly with a serious look on their face and two "golden" medals pinned on their chest. *Ah... this one is because I am now eighty, and the other is to commemorate the fiftieth anniversary of the victory over Germany* – explains the veteran of time. *Oh yes, you can take a photograph of us... please.*

A young Russian woman who now works for an American oil company in Kazakhstan heard my story and came over – *you should have been on this train in the early 1990's when Kazakhstan declared independence! Masses of Russians were going back to Russia at that time, and Kazakhs were returning. An unbelievable mass of people was travelling on these trains... all three layers of bunks were used; men with women or other men - total strangers - slept squashed two to a bunk; people slept on the floor, on the table, slept sitting or standing if they couldn't find space on a bunk; you had to walk over people's bodies sometimes stepping on them to get to the samovar for a drop of water; couldn't get to the WC - not that you would want to anyway seeing its state. Ticket inspectors gave up – they couldn't get through the mass of people, and tempers flared easily. If you didn't have enough food or drink – you just had to do without it. This is luxury in comparison! Here's my company's address – come and visit us when you are in town.*

Hell, if the state of the trains in the 1990's is already history, and travelling *platz-card* today is a relative luxury, where will I ever find an opportunity to experience the depth of misery of *nasi chłopcy* or the *"wsie Polaki amnestirovani"* from Jan's *lagier*!

Day one, two… and the wheels of my train turn round and round… and it's turning out to be a friendly and interesting trip. A young man of about nineteen couldn't resist the opportunity: *you are from England, aren't you? I have just done my two years national service in the Russian navy on the Barents Sea – absolutely great; we had such thorough training!* And, indeed, doesn't he have all the answers to the politics of the 2nd World War, the sacrifice of the Russian people, the rapacious and lying West and, quite frankly, I have some difficulty in parrying his blows, perhaps due to my inadequate Russian. Fortunately, the train was coming into a station and the young man cut his recitation short, put on his Navy uniform and, facing the public, proudly acknowledged their looks of approval and handclapping with a broad smile. He got off, and I got off here too to supplement my tomato, cucumber and bread.

Numerous vendors were ready for us on the platform with baskets and bags full of home cooked pasties, boiled eggs, fish, vegetables, beverages and the like. Many passengers wouldn't risk coming out onto the platform or leave their things unattended and bought what they could through carriage windows, but the "boss" watched the time and shepherded us all back into his wagon... No one missed the train, and the wheels of my train went round and round again till the next scheduled stop at some distant railway station.

And those trains packed with the amnestied Poles also made frequent but unscheduled and unannounced stops along the line, usually somewhere on the sidings or a long way from the station. No one could be sure how long they would have to wait – a day or perhaps two, an hour, or only a few minutes, for all train schedules, all trains, all engines and even carriages yielded priority to the demands of the War, or the bungling of the planning system and the incompetence of its operators. But when their train did stop, volunteers or delegates from amongst the miserable occupants rushed out to find some bread, get a bucket of *kipiatok* and bring it back to those outstretched hands.

And what if the steam whistle blew, or if it didn't, and the wheels of the train began to roll and those out to get bread or *kipiatok* didn't make it back to the train in time? Their journey to the Anders Army is full of such incidents, of tragedies, of families separated for ever, of broken hearts, deaths... And yet, there were many happy endings; somehow those left behind managed to get onto another train going in the same direction, to catch up, to meet up with their travel companions at the next station or town down the line. And even in these dismal conditions the young were somehow able to capture moments of happiness, be it a kiss or cuddle on the buffers, or love in an empty side-lined cattle truck, or in a quiet place by the rail tracks… if only they would hear that steam whistle in time.

Aralsk

Their trains, like mine today, stopped at Aralsk where from the windows of the train they could see the blue waters of the Aral Sea; and passengers would rush to buy fish and whatever other provisions they could find here. But today, clusters of men stand idly on the platform, and only I and one or two other men get off and walk towards the station building.

A forlorn, shabby station on the main rail route from Moscow to Tashkent; it looks even less inviting inside but I am stunned by the huge mural on one wall of the waiting room. Evidently, Lenin saw that Aralsk held out a great promise; he spelt it out in his Directive, and his concordat with the people of Aralsk is enshrined in this huge mural, still on the same wall, still in vibrant brown, yellow and blue colours depicting fishermen in the image of Lenin himself at work – spellbinding by its size and great energy. Aralsk's commitment couldn't be clearer:

> "LENIN'S 4th DIRECTIVE - WE WILL DELIVER 14 WAGONS OF FISH"

Lenin had faith in people; Stalin had faith in rapid industrialization. Then came Khrushchev; he had faith in *kolkhozes* and in cotton – the white gold. He had the waters of the Amu Daria siphoned off to irrigate cotton fields and water melons in Uzbekistan, and starved the Aral Sea of its source. The Aral Sea shrunk; its fishing fleet now rests scavenged on the sand at the bottom of the dry sea; fish processing plants closed; the people of Aralsk lost their livelihood; its population shrank; the environment turned into desert, and salt dust storms eat out people's lungs.

And where are the Kazakhs now? A two-hour ride in a packed minibus takes me way out into the steppe – to Zhizhaga - no longer a *kolkhoz* but a Kazakh village. Within a minute of my getting out of the minibus all passengers have disappeared. The camel resting in the middle of the main track through the village spits at this strange intruder as I pass him, a cow stands immobile on the rooftop of a shack gazing longingly at the desert, perhaps dreaming of green pastures; three big-horned cattle laze in the shade of a single tree… no other soul or living things in sight. I am alone, stranded. I walk up to the cemetery on a hill to while away two hours as I wait, hopefully, for the returning minibus - no Polish graves here, no Christian crosses, one marked with Stalin's Red Star, a surprisingly large number of Moslem graves… Kazakh lives must be short here for, quite evidently, this is not a very old or large settlement. A sad view of the village below -

houses like pebbles sit in a sea of sand and salt pans - nothing moves, nothing lives…

Perhaps I am a resented intruder here too, for sudden gusts of wind from behind the cemetery penetrate several rows of graves and begin to blow swirling sand and salt dust in my face and, just as suddenly, the village down below seems to come to life – surely, I am seeing a mounted Kazakh corralling horses! But at this very moment the wind gets really aggressive; it wants me to throw me out - now! Everything dissolves in a swirling cloud of sand and salt dust - the Kazakh, the horses, the entire village - all. I know the way back is downhill and find my way to the village – blind.

And my train from Aralsk starts to roll on and on again.

<u>Krasnyy Most – Sarkyrama</u>

I carry in my mind a story of the unimaginable suffering in Stalin's "Garden of Eden" so well told by Witold Janda in his book *Dotrwać do Świtu* [To survive till dawn]. Back in 1942, our family could well have been amongst this group of amnestied Polish people trekking two hundred kilometres across the wild steppe from Arys to Sarkyrama where they hoped to find work, food and roof over their heads. I can almost feel their ordeal - always thirsty, always on the point of starvation, night after night sleeping under open skies, often drenched to the skin with rain, knee-deep in mud, exhausted, yet still having to help the Kazakh and his oxen pull the *arba* out of mud up to the axel of its huge six-foot wooden wheels. And on days like today, when the sun beats down mercilessly, they were equally drenched to the skin, but with sweat; as always thirsty, as always on the point of starvation, they steadied the *arba* while it jostled the women, children, the sick and the baggage, and prayed it would not overturn. They made it to Ekipinde – just. A night's rest in a shack but under a roof, resuscitated with a bowl of thick soup, then on across the bridge over the river Bogen… only another twenty kilometres to go.

What a sight that Polish group must have been on entering Sarkyrama; the Kazakhs living in such remote places had probably never seen people "bleached" so white, blond hair, blue eyes, strange clothes; village dogs had never smelt that smell.

I got off the train at Arys, a busy railway station on the main line to Tashkent, and I was lucky on that day – the only bus leaving Ares that day was going in the right direction.

And I too made it to Ekipinde. Now it is called *Krasnyy Most* - Red Bridge. I have been spellbound before, but here, I stood by an abandoned little red bridge and shook my head in disbelief! So much has changed over the past seventy years - my life, their life, Stalin's legacy demolished… but this little red bridge still spans the Bogen. True, Stalin's blood-red colour has faded, and its steel girders sag a little. True, I cannot cross it as its planks are loose or missing, but it still stands there like a marker in the painful history of the Polish families that came here. Its mellowed red colours contrast gently with perfectly blue skies, the deep blue of the river, and the pale green of its banks; and on the far side of the bridge, a track of sun-baked clay leads back into the endless steppe from whence they came. No *arba* wobbles in its deep ruts today, no cattle, no pain, no misery... just infinity.

Perhaps in 1942 *Krasnyy Most* had greater importance for it stood at the intersection of two major tracts - but today, it is no more than a bus stop on a road somewhere in the steppe. A row of several trading stalls and eating places, a petrol station, a parking lot off the road, one public well for drinking water... taxis and their drivers crowding the intersection, several dwellings in the background and swirls of dust as vehicles go past – that's all. No hotel or any kind of lodgings here, and it's not like in Uzbekistan where people welcome you into their houses. Not much of a welcome for me; not quite the place for an old man with a rucksack.

The café-owner looks at me with more suspicion than curiosity – a traveller from England, really? Not the unshaven vagabond I look - truly? But he relents, if only a little - *O.K. rest and spend the night on the veranda outside*. But as curious individuals come up to this stranger and talk, my host casts me a second glance and upgrades me – *sit in the coolness of the café inside and have some tea*. As we talk, at first perfunctorily, I buy two bears and, wow, I am upgraded again – I can lie down and rest in the reception room. And as the day turns to evening and more people show an interest in the stranger, and talk... I deserved another upgrade – I can sleep in the state-room - I sigh with relief! But just as I start spreading out my belongings, his wife rushes in – *come out, come out... an order for a big reception has just come in, we need the room*! Of course! It is the 9th of May 2010 - the 65th Anniversary of Russian Victory in the war for the Motherland - for the Kazakhs it's their Independence Day.

What a relief for the owners of the café; they thought orders would never come this year, but now guests roll in – one in an invalid's chair – and their faces are beaming. Suddenly, a large group of youths descends on the café – a party! Dancing to blaring modern music - none of the traditional Kazakh strings and songs; young, lithe bodies swing to Western tunes. I take photographs of the milling crowd; the dancers pose delighted, and the owners are delighted too!

When this is all over, I am invited to take supper with them at the kitchen table – the ultimate upgrade! The whole family sits down: grandmother, brother and the young couple – the owners. All happy, smiling and delighted with the day; we share the food on the table; why use forks or spoons when we can equally well eat with fingers from two communal plates... Talk, talk and talk, and I can see the wistful look in the young wife's eyes – she has been to Almaty and Astana but oh, how she would like to travel, to see the world... No, it is not easy for them. They are leasing this café - two years now - and that costs 9000 Tenge per month; and even here, they feel the recession; and winter months are particularly difficult. Finally, it's time to retire – the owner and me to the state-room where two mats and rugs have been spread for us on the floor; the others retire to their house nearby.

I have in my mind a picture from Witold Janda's book – a waterfall on the fast-flowing Bogen in Sarkyrama, huts of mud on the high bank of the river, and fields of swaying wheat... It could have been an idyllic place to live if only the *kolkhoz* had not been turned into Stalin's "Garden of Eden". There was no "milk and honey" here in 1942; the corrupt bosses lived quite well while others, like the Poles, were destitute and on the brink of constant starvation in the winter months, and many died from extreme exhaustion or disease... and nobody cared.

The Bogen flows today as it did then but, I am told, the waterfall is gone! How could a waterfall just disappear? But it did! It was blown up for some reason, and as the mud huts disintegrated with time, the village moved further west. A Hajji, in flowing white robes, leads my host and me to where the waterfall once was - only seven kilometres from the *kolkhoz* along a track across open fields, but it took us more than half hour by car! And that was long enough for the Hajji to try to make a Moslem of me. The advantages were obvious – he has two wives, they work to keep him... why, he sleeps with one, one night, sleeps with the other the next night, so they can't complain! He is fifty, and happy... and that little urchin playing in the yard is his youngest! Being a good Moslem, he went on the Hajj to Mecca last year by coach – that cost him $1500 which he had to save over several years - but that's the obligation of every Moslem, and now, he can call himself Hajji, wear flowing white robes, and expect respect from all. But, notwithstanding the enticement of two wives, I had to cut short his proselytizing for, at the moment, I was only interested in history – in 1942.

The heavy spring rains had stopped and the sun had shone all the previous week so the ground had time to dry out and we were now on a track of rock-hard mud full of deep potholes and deep ruts gauged out by vehicle tyres. As our car moved at snail's pace and was often on the point of tipping over onto its side while the bottom of the petrol tank levelled the ground, the logic behind the huge, six-foot high wooden wheels on *arbas* became quite obvious.

Yes... the mud huts that once stood on the high escarpment are gone, the water fall is gone, but the Bogen is as enchanting today as it must have been then – cool, perfectly clean, inviting. Its water shimmers in the bright sunshine as it ripples in a broad arc set in pastel green of the meadows on its left bank. Its meandering is constrained by the riverbank on the other side - high and hard but radiating the warmth of the loess profusely covered with bushes flowering in a mass of pale violet. And to the southeast, several hundred kilometres away, loom the majestic, magnificent peaks of Tien-Shan shrouded in purple haze... a beautiful, serene spot on earth. But much closer, only a hundred yards or so, on that high ridge by the river, rests a cemetery – a painful reminder. And there, amongst its graves rests Witold's mother... and memories of those painful and tragic years: 1941, 2, 3, 4, 5 and 6... so many.

But even my host couldn't resist the Bogen and, stripped to his underpants, jumped in for a swim... so refreshing, so clean, so cold. Time to go; I leave reluctantly. Back in *Krasnyy Most*, my host treats me to a farewell lunch of delicious fish taken from the Bogen - just for me, fried just for me; and when we part, I hear – *come again*...

Tashkent – YangiYul

...and it's still a long way from Arys to Tashkent. A massive earthquake in 1966 destroyed much of the city of Tashkent and little of its early heritage remained intact. The city has been rebuilt on a grand scale since Uzbekistan's independence and, as in Moscow, hotels have been upgraded to 5-star quality and shock with their room prices. But there are other options too.

A woman met in the street finds me a "place" at the back of the best hotel – 4 men stripped to their underpants are snoring at noon in one room, but stepping over their bodies, I can enter a cubby-hole with my "bed" and a broken window to let in air... and dogs. Seeing my passport the price of the room doubled instantly but it's still cheap... and well below the quality of the *platz-card* cubicles which helps to empathise with the plight of the amnestied Poles.

A good straight road leads to YangiYul. It's already hot in early May and the stalls along much of the road exiting Tashkent are piled high with strawberries. A bus takes me down this "strawberry lane" into YngiYul, but look as I may, I find nothing to remind me of the Anders Army. The river still flows through the town as it did in 1942 but the military camps on its bank have gone, the rows and rows of white tents have gone; the town has exploded in size and population, and the orchards that bloomed so beautifully in May 1942 have been banished to the outskirts. The train station is still here and parts of the station building could well be the same that welcomed the Army. A local man tells me that a big building in the town centre has been demolished not so long ago – perhaps that was the Army H.Q.

But step into the bazar and you enter a different world. That proverbial land "flowing with milk and honey" that the amnestied people had hoped to find here is actually on display - stacks of fruit, vegetables, meat, bread enough to satiate the 5,000 and more. Life throbs, girls come out from behind the stalls to pose for photographs; an old man wants his photo taken hoping that his digital or paper image will live longer than he. But this apparent contentment goes hand in hand with obvious poverty, yet there is no evident anger on peoples' faces… only the mules and donkeys tied up along the wall bare their teeth and bite their neighbours out of frustration and anger at the bad treatment by their owners.

And yet, in 1942, this land of fruit and honey was the land of pestilence. People died like flies from plagues as if sent from heaven to punish those already suffering – typhoid, malaria, scarlet fever or from utter exhaustion on their walk from Stalin's *lagiers* to the Army. The only hope of salvation was to get out with the Army, and quickly. My father and our family did; we got onto the train taking the amnestied Polish people across the Karakum desert to Ashgabat and Krasnovodsk in Turkmenistan, then across the Caspian Sea to Pahlavi in Persia – the door to salvation. Pity those that didn't...

Kagan, the doorway to Bukhara - August 1942. It's hot - very hot. A mass of people in rags swirls around Kagan railway station; at every turn Polish people waiting for that train that will get them out of the land of the *lagier*, *posiolek*, starvation, pestilence and death... waiting for the train that for many will never come.

A mother and her three small children, exhausted, hungry and thirsty, sit in the sand outside the station. They would have made a complete family if only their father was there too... Chin on chest, eyes staring blankly at the sand, their thoughts were slowly revolving around one, single question: where are you dad... husband? The last time they saw him was on 28th August 1939 - the day general mobilization; just three days later Hitler attacked Poland - and then Stalin... three long and terrible years ago. Where is he now... dead or alive, or felling trees in the *lagiers* of Archangelsk, or in the gold or uranium mines of Kolyma? Or perhaps, at this very moment, he is making his way to the Polish Army in Tashkent. Or - oh God... no! Perhaps dead from sickness or exhaustion, like thousands of other men, women and children, now buried in cemeteries in Uzbekistan, Kazakhstan, Russia. Or perhaps buried in Ghuzar or Kanimekh or in one of the many other Polish cemeteries now sprouting in this region?

They are not alone. The station is crowded with people just like them - Polish men, women, children, and soldiers, all feeling lost. They were dumped here from the train and no one knew what next; questions and worries raced in their mind: will the NKVD provide food; will they be looked after by Polish organizations; where is this Polish Army - the gateway to life, to freedom... to Poland? One thing everybody knew; they had learnt the "first commandment" in Stalin's "Garden of Eden" the hard way - you don't work, you don't eat - equally applicable to men, women, the aged or infirm, and babies. But what could they do - only sit and wait.

A day later, they are still waiting when an extraordinary scene unfolds before their eyes. A cavalcade of Uzbeks appears in the evening with strange carts they call *arba*, and they all settle themselves down for the night at the station. In the morning, the railway station becomes a beehive of activity reminiscent of the slave trade in Bukhara. The Uzbeks look the people over, target the strongest and offer work in *kolkhozes*.

For this family that train to freedom was not coming, so what choice had they? They had to eat and needed shelter from the scorching sun in summer and the bitter cold in winter. A Kazakh may take them on his *arba* on a two hundred kilometre trek through the open steppe to *Krasnyy Most* and then on to work in a *kolkhoz in* Ekipinde, or an Uzbek will lead them to a *kolkhoz* in Alkatyn, or some other place lost in the far away desert... to remain there forever in unmarked and forgotten graves. Only the young will perhaps get a second chance.

Kagan - May 2010. It's hot - already very hot. You wouldn't have guessed that you are at a railway station but for those huge letters on the impressive grey marble façade of the building spelling "VOKZAL". No, there are no trains to or from Kagan to Ekipinde or Ghuzar but a private car will take me to the Ghuzar cemetery.

Ghuzar

In the summer of 1942, it was hot in Ghuzar too - very hot; what water there was was foul and spreading disease. Several thousand Polish men, women and children came here in the hope of deliverance from the hands of the NKVD. Able-bodied men and women hoped to join the Polish Army in Tashkent; civilians hoped to escape from Stalin's "Garden of Eden" alongside the Army, but in the meantime, they needed food and a roof over their heads. They found themselves dispersed in numerous local villages and transit camps - waiting, hoping, dying from exhaustion and disease.

There were many transit camps in the Tashkent region, but Ghuzar had the "distinction" of hosting the greatest number of deaths - 697 men, women and children perished here within a period of two-three months! Townsfolk call the cemetery where they are buried "Polachki" - "that Polish place". It is a depressing and dust-covered small town today.

The gate to "Polachki" is locked but already, disappointment, sadness and anger well in my mind. What is this? All I see is a number of long "horticultural test beds" of orange-coloured sandy soil still un-seeded, and fenced in to keep out trespassers? 675 Christians lie buried here, yet not a single cross is visible? A black marble tablet with names of the dead cut into it extends close to the ground; a few trees alongside provide some shade, and a pillar of grey sandstone with a barely visible Polish eagle and inscription... is that all? Is that the biggest concession the Polish Government could wring out of the Uzbeks? If only this place had been left just as it was at the beginning - mounds of earth overgrown with grass, or even just a heap of soil and just one cross - one cross! That would have made a much bigger impact; it would stir memories; it would stir one's conscience. Why "beautify" it; why sanitize it beyond any meaning or spiritual impact?

The guard - *ohrona* - of "Polachki" unlocks the gate and explains that this place was chosen for burial because here the soil is softer, so it was easier to dig graves in winter. The consecration of the cemetery was a big affair he tells me – *a man in flowing white robes came, many delegates from Poland came, and many Uzbek officials; the entire place was sealed off by police. Local people were kept well away, not even the one local woman of Polish descent who wanted to help in some way was allowed to participate.*

It's still only early afternoon but I am now no longer in the mood to travel any further today; *ohrona* will put me up in his house just across the road from the entrance to the cemetery.

If I had come two weeks later, *ohrona* would have treated me to a spectacle I would remember – he is marrying off his son. He and his wife thought the daughter of his wife's sister would make a goof wife for their son, but it was not a foregone decision. So they arranged a discrete mutual viewing for the young somewhere in the bazaar – *Well son… what do you think of that girl? Well mother… you know… you always know best. If you think so… yes, I will marry her…*

But even within the circle of quite close relatives, tradition must be upheld and fees paid – *ohrona* has already put down a deposit for the bride-to-be: four sheep, plus sixty kilos of rice, plus two kilos of butter, plus a huge number of *lepioshka* (flat bread), plus other items. *Oh, by the way,* says *ohrona* looking at me with some apprehension, *we don't drink alcohol here… so if you want some, you will have to buy it for yourself.*

The newly-weds will share the house with *ohrona* and the rest of the family until a separate dwelling will be ready for them, so for the time being, there's plenty of room for a guest like me; he is happy to sleep in the porch where the air is cooler in the night. There is practically no furniture in the house other than sleeping mattresses on floors and one small table, barely off the floor, on which food is served. The entire wealth of the household seems to be rolled up in carpets and colourful rugs stacked high on chests against the walls. They create a warm atmosphere where it's easy to forget my anger on seeing *Polachki*.

The house is quietly shaded with mulberry trees and their maggot-like fruits are collected on a canvas under the tree – nothing goes to waste. Water is scarce – a meagre well supplies all their needs; a ewer stands by its side to pour a few drops of water for washing hands and general ablutions. In the field beyond the gate, several black sheep roam freely – perhaps they are his real wealth.

Later, after a simple meal, while relaxing in the cool evening air, our conversation reverts to marriage, and... girls! *You know, there are many girls here in town... of course, it is forbidden for Moslems, but they need to earn some money to pay for education... They will do anything you want... in your room or in the hotel... anything, and they are young and beautiful - some are only just fifteen... Do you want one* - he asks.

Do I want one! No alcohol but I can have a girl instead!

I slept well that night on *ohrona's* mattress in a room full of striking carpets stacked up to the ceiling. What spoilt the moment, as I woke, was the view from the window – the early morning sunshine was streaming in directly from the cemetery, from those "horticultural test beds". I had to see the cemetery again, this time alone.

Of course! There... a cross! In fact I see now there is a cross on each of the communal graves - but it lies flat on blocks of sandstone laid almost horizontally, and hence is not very conspicuous. But surely, I couldn't have missed them yesterday, so why was I so angry, so upset, so negative? Perhaps it's because of the mental picture I still carry with me of the cemetery in Mławka, in Poland. There, German soldiers who were killed on Polish soil in the 1914 and 1939 Wars lie interred; the same Germans who launched the two holocausts, who killed and murdered thousands... and for them - well over 14,000 of them - a magnificent cemetery on Polish soil! Hundreds of crosses, grey marble pillars with engraved names... all in a sombre environment, in peace, in silence, never to be forgotten... as if they made the ultimate sacrifice for freedom!

And here? Here, "Polachki" - the victims of the Nazi and Soviet invaders, lie in "that Polish Place" - a place where I can't get vodka to drown my sorrow, but I can have a girl!

That black marble tablet in the cemetery was riveting though; the rows and rows of Polish names cut into it were too many to read but I knew my father's name was not amongst them. He survived, but I wonder just how close he must have been to joining them. Pity I never asked, or listened... that only now I am trying to understand.

Understand! How can I ever "understand" a man who had to walk the "Valley of Death" in Murmansk; had to compete for food with rats; had to run the gauntlet of the sea journey like Jan; had to live with the label "*tut washa moghila*". And at the exit from "Stalin's Evil Empire", on the threshold of freedom, when hope was rekindled, had to witness hundreds of men women and children, emaciated and sick as he himself must have been - dying... and the thought gnawing his mind that his own wife and children might, perhaps, be somewhere there amongst them... or already in those shallow graves along that road to freedom, perhaps even here, in that "Polachki" place.

How can I "understand" a man who at the end of his GULAG trail had to embark on the bitter road to exile? When on the way to battle for the freedom of Italy, rumours were swirling that his supposedly best friends, Mr Churchill and President Roosevelt, had acquiesced to the division of Poland along the Curzon line, and earmarked his Homeland for Stalin at the Tehran Conference in December 1943? And then, just before he goes into battle he learns that this man, Stalin, now a "great friend" of the Allies, had some 12,000 Polish officers murdered in cold blood, 4,000 of whom lie buried in the pits of Katyń?

It was easy for the Allies to pin the highest military and civil orders on the chest of General Anders and to decorate his generals, but while basking in the glory of the victory at Monte Cassino, the cause they were all fighting for – the freedom of their Homeland - was somehow side-lined. Yalta confirmed their suspicions – indeed, Polish territory east of the Curzon line, was ceded to Stalin! Yet Polish armed forces continued to fight at the side of the Allies; they kept their promise and fought on to liberate Italy… took part in the Normandy landings and closed the Falaise Gap, and fought to liberate Belgium and Holland. They fought on till the final victory over the German foe. And at the end of the victorious War, they were not invited to participate in the Victory Parade in London – political expediency got in the way.

And what do I know about war - nothing but the words I have read and the insight my trail has shared with me. But, my father was in the 5th Kresowa Infantry Division; he fought at Monte Cassino…

perhaps taking part in that mad scramble uphill in the middle of the night to take the crest of the Phantom Ridge... where he could have been blown up in the minefields, or torn apart by enemy artillery and mortars, or shot to pieces by frontal and flanking machinegun fire from German bunkers perfectly blended into the terrain...

How can I ever "understand" what men must have been living through in the last few hours before that whistle blew, and the scars this must have left on the mind? Was my father perhaps like that tough young man at his side, crying, his body shaking as if in the grip of malaria, so evidently ashamed of his state of mind but the fear of death was uncontrollable? Or was he like some others who ate all their provisions at once for, in their view, no one should go to work or battle on an empty stomach; or like those men who with gravity and professionalism inspected their rifles; or was he sitting on a rock, a photograph on his knee, scribbling his last few words of love and goodbye... or was he just sitting there, head bowed, his rifle between his legs, mind blank, numb, waiting for his fate?"[7]

No doubt psychiatrists and psychologists will claim to "understand"; no doubt they have some suitable jargon, but how can I ever "understand"? My father was a military man - a man in "khaki and black beret". In his eyes, in the years immediately after the war, I never could walk upright enough, never could do the squats properly, never could do anything well enough.

But he did find us! He must have searched all over Russia and Kazakhstan at the time of joining the Anders Army - and he found us! And I was born a second time, for when he pulled us out of that hell-hole in Kazakhstan to which our family was deported in 1940 I must have been near-death. It was almost exactly three years from that fateful day in August 1939 when he left his baby son and a long eight years later when that man in "khaki and black beret" walked back into my life again – and by then I was in the UK…

Those early years in the UK were difficult transition years… years when any job he could get would be so great to have. I remember his coming home from work with W.C. French stamped on his gumboots and on his coat. I was always there, eagerly waiting to pull his boots off, to unwrap his feet… surreptitiously searching for that cold fried egg sandwich mother had made him for lunch… that he would keep for me because he knew I loved it!

How could I hold his military mustering of me against him? But I did… until very much later. But, at the age of just eight, he was a stranger to me; gradually, he became a man who, in my eyes, could do anything. He could make soles for my shoes from car tyres, take junked furniture apart and make new furniture for our home… He would bring a grey envelope with his weekly wages and, with a proud and loving smile, give it to my mother - whole, unopened - no beer money or cigarette money kept aside for himself. What better sign of total trust in his wife? And he was a man respected by others in the community - I could see that, even at the age of eight!

And he didn't forget Wielowieś; he didn't abandon his family in Poland - and there were many of them - two brothers and five sisters still alive. When Poland opened up, even just a little, he wrote to them often. They needed help; and I remember many packs - 25kg. and larger - of food and clothes, or parcels of medicines going to Poland. There were times when my father could help only so much but many in communist Poland thought that England was overflowing with milk and honey… while for us, back in the 1950's and 60's, life was tough.

And when, at long last, I knocked on the door of my cousins, in Wielowieś and Ostrów, I could see he was remembered well. His kind letters and parcels gave them hope knowing that they had not been forgotten.

Yes! He was my Daddy, just the way he was, "understood" or perhaps "misunderstood" in my own child's way.

I thank God he survived those dreadful years of war, only a pity that he died too soon. The footprints he and the many thousands of other men and women left in the land of "Stalin's Evil Empire" are fading into history but they will forever remain fresh in my memory, as will that one disquieting question – what would I have done… what kind of a man would I have become?

And somewhere, amongst the many thousands of Polish graves in Konimech, Karmana, Jakkbog,

Czirakczi, Szachrizabz, Kitab, Olmazar, YangiYul, or in the thousands of *kolkhozes* across Russia, Kazakhstan and Uzbekistan; in Tehran and Isfahan, or in one of those unmarked graves along the railway tracks… is the grave of my little sister, RIP 1942. Aged only seven….

How she must have been waiting for her daddy, overcome by unbearable pain - Mommy… where's Daddy… Daddy? How our mother's heart must have ached, but what could she say, how could she explain to her little girl that her Daddy had to go to fight the Germans, but he will be back! He will be back… to take her back home… back to her doggy, her toys… Surely, this loveable little girl will "understand".

Epilogue

One day, back at home in London, and quite out of the blue, an email appeared on my computer screen from an organization in Russia dealing with the issues of mass murder of Polish officers in Katyń. It was an extract from NKVD official sources relating to my father's whereabouts in 1939-1941. It stated:

Name:	Kubica	Józef
Father's Name:	Kubica	Franciszek
Date of Birth:	1900	
Arrested in Lithuania	1939/09/19	Zawiasy
Prison Camp:	1940/07/41	Kozielsk
Prison Camp:	1941/05/16	Ponoi
	1941/07/27	
Anders:	1941/09/04	Tatiszczewo

So it was Ponoi! Indeed, only a "miracle" could have saved my father from sure death in this *lagier*; and the "miracle" did happen!

And the wheels in my heart and mind now go on... and on... and on... repeating: *come again... come again... come again...* Perhaps *Klawdiya Elinskaya* will still be waiting for me in Murmansk, the gangway down...

And, at last, I have received information about Grave #511 in a cemetery in Tehran, the name on it is S†P Alicja Kubica, 1935 + 1942 R.i.P. - my little sister! How she must have been waiting the past seventy years for her little brother to come, to say hello, to remember... and I will come.

Murmansk, Revda – railway line built by prisoners

The old route - *etap* to GULAG-72km.

GULAG-72km. the ovens

GULAG-72km.

Kirovsk mine

Kirovsk, beautiful nature - polluted mine lagoon

Kazakhstan, Kingir Rudnik *lagier*

Kazakhstan, Kingir Rudnik *lagier* – the pit

Kingir Rudnik – burial ground

Karaganda, Spaask – burial ground

Sources and Works Cited

1. Orłowski Jan, Major in the 2nd Polish Corps, extracts selected and translated by the author from his unpublished memoirs with kind permission of his son Rafał Orłowski.

2. Extracts from the answer to author's question posed on the "Kresy-Siberia Foundation" Blog https://groups.yahoo.com/neo/groups/Kresy-Siberia/info

3. Konarski F. / Ref Ren/ *Piosenki z Plecaka Helenki,* published by Ref Ren 1946

4. Orłowski Jan (see 1 above)

5. Konarski F. / Ref Ren/ (see 3 above)

6. This scenario is partially sourced from - Wernik Romuald, *Białe Noce i Czarne Dnie*

7. Kubica Jerry *Footprints on Monte Cassino*

Bibliography

1. Kizny Tomasz, *GULAG Life and Death in Soviet Concentration Camps*, Firefly Books 2004

2. Pawłowska Teresa, *Moje Powojenne Łagry* „Stella Maris" Gdańsk 1992

3. Grzywacz Bernard, *Krąg Workuta*, Archiwum Wschodnie, Warszawa 2004

4. O. Janocha Albin, OFM Cap, *Pod Opieką Matki Bożej*, Polskie Towarzystwo Ludoznawcze, Wrocław 1993

5. Żaroń Piotr, *Obozy Jeńców polskich w ZSSR w latach 1939-1941*, UNICORN Publishing Studio 1994

6. Czapski Józef, *Na Nieludzkiej Ziemi*, Wydawnictwo Znak, Kraków 2001

7. Janda Witold, *Dotrwać do Świtu*, Wydawnictwo Adam Marszałek, Toruń 1998

8. Wernik Romuald, *Białe Noce i Czarne Dnie*, Polska Fundacja Kulturalna, 1987

9. "Memorial" www.memo.ru/eng

10. Ivan Vdovin & Sergei Ganusievich, *Russian Lapland 1996*, info@ruslapland.ru

11. Kubica Jerry, *Footprints on Monte Cassino*

Printed in Dunstable, United Kingdom